# Stories in Faith

Exploring Our
Unitarian Universalist Principles and Sources
Through Wisdom Tales

Gail Forsyth-Vail

Tracey L. Hurd
Developmental Editor

UNITARIAN UNIVERSALIST ASSOCIATION

BOSTON

Printed in the United States.

ISBN 1-55896-528-9
978-1-55896-528-7

Library of Congress Cataloging-in-Publication Data

Forsyth-Vail, Gail.
   Stories in faith : exploring our UU principles and sources through wisdom tales / Gail Forsyth-Vail ; Tracey L. Hurd, developmental editor.
      p. cm.
   ISBN-13: 978-1-55896-528-7 (pbk. : alk. paper)
   ISBN-10: 1-55896-528-9 (pbk. : alk. paper)  1. Unitarian Universalist Association.  I. Hurd, Tracey L. II. Title.
   BX9841.3.F67 2007
   289.1'32--dc22
                                    2007011944

09 08 07
5 4 3 2 1

The following publishers have generously given permission to abridge stories from copyrighted works. "We Are One" is a selection from the book *The Rainbow People*, text copyright © 1989 by Laurence Yep, used by permission of HarperCollins Publishers. "The Green Man" is an abridgment from the book *The Green Man*, text copyright © 1979 by Gail E. Haley, used by permission of Gail E. Haley.

# Contents

# Preface

We are shaped by stories. This book, written for parents, teachers, religious educators, ministers, and spiritual seekers, explores how we are called to stories and why they touch our souls. It presents nineteen soul-stirring tales from the seven Principles and six Sources of our Unitarian Universalist tradition. These wisdom tales offer us the journeys of folklore or scriptural heroes, the magnificence of the natural world, and inspiration from the lives of prophets, teachers, explorers, and dreamers. Each offers a way for us to examine our own lives and navigate how we are called to live our faith in the world.

Each wisdom tale is presented with information about its origins or cultural context, modeling the respectful use of diverse stories upon which our faith is based. Insight particular to Unitarian Universalist faith is provided for each story, with attention to the themes of hearing a calling, opening to new revelation, and finding wisdom through the Principles and Sources. This structure provides the reader or seeker with new ways to know the stories and grow in faith. In addition, the book provides ideas for extending exploration of the stories in congregational settings or at home.

The book provides stories that captivate and enrich us, stories that we will want to read again and again. And it provides timeless wisdom, which can be known only through stories that help us on our journey of Unitarian Universalist faith.

Tracey Hurd

# Why Stories?

People throughout the ages and across cultures love stories. We are collectors and tellers of stories—about our own lives, our world, and those who came before. We find new meaning in creating and sharing stories. They bring communities together and transmit collective wisdom about large questions of identity and values.

Our human capacity for self-awareness and wonder is both a gift and challenge. We know that whatever our present circumstances, life has not *always* been as it is now. From our earliest years, we ponder the beginnings of our world and the universe, the wonder and beauty that surround us, the tales of our ancestors, and the lives of others with whom we share the planet. As social beings, we want to be with others. Groups—families, neighborhoods, faith communities, and other circles of love and caring—give us a sense of home from which to explore the world and the mystery of being human. We are eager to know the rituals, symbols, understandings, and values that identify our groups. We share our understandings of what it means to be human in groups, and storytelling is a primary vehicle for this sharing.

Stories reflect the wisdom and experience of the community. They are meant to be told and retold. We hold them in our hearts to help us respond to the wonder and the challenge of living. It is precisely because they are familiar and repeated that we can mine ever deeper meaning from them.

Each Christmas, many of us hear anew the Jesus nativity story. Some years, the message that resonates is the angel's "Fear not!" Other years, it is the journey of the young couple in search of shelter, or the idea of hope born in the most unexpected of places. One time we may hear the Exodus story told during Passover, and it may help us recognize the wilderness journeys in our own lives. Another year the same story may spur us to remember to think about freedom from tyranny as a birthright of all people. The story of the blind men and the elephant may remind us of the limitations of our personal perspective, or it may challenge us to explore new ideas beyond our own experience.

Knowing these stories well helps us connect them with our own lives. Stories remind us of who we are and what we value. They become part of our individual spiritual toolkits, available to us whenever we need them.

When we hear a familiar story, it is not the single unadorned telling of the tale we hear. Our minds and spirits vibrate with overtones from other times we have heard the story and meanings it has already brought to our lives. When we hear the Christmas story, the Exodus story, or the story of the blind men and the elephant, we bring to the experience not just our present selves but also our memories of the other times when we have heard the story. We are at once a three-year-old hearing the story for the first time, a seven-year-old who reads it in a picture book, a ten-year-old who acts out the story, a teenager wondering if the story has anything to offer, a young adult seeking a path, a person with a heavy heart, and a person on the precipice of a new adventure. Our memories of previous encounters with the story are liminal tones that add depth to its repetition. They enable us to better access wisdom from the story that fits our current circumstances.

We all have family and community stories we share, lighthearted and funny, warm and touching, sad, or frightening. We remember the birth of a child, the rush to the hospital with a broken arm, the holiday fair when it snowed all day, and the good-bye service for a beloved elder. We tell those stories over and over, creating a sculpture of shared memory out of bits and pieces of images, feelings, and words. There are bigger stories as well: ones that speak of journeys, both temporal and spiritual. These tales—of courage and weakness, triumph and loss, joy and sorrow, curiosity and challenge, call and response—are told again and again, not only because they are engaging, but also because they nourish us as they have nourished the generations before us. Wisdom stories offer the opportunity for dialogue between the past and the present.

Unitarian Universalism is a living tradition. We believe that revelation is neither fixed nor complete; there is much more spiritual truth yet to be discovered. One of the ways we discover this truth is in the dialogue between stories of the past and challenges of the present. Through this process, new discoveries are made, resulting in fresh understandings of our faith. Stories acquire overtones, for tellers and listeners, that give insights into life's meaning and purpose. We deepen our faith journeys both as individuals and as communities bound by a covenant that calls us to accept, encourage, and challenge one another to spiritual growth and faith development.

What makes a story a wisdom tale? Simply put, a wisdom tale is one that bears repeating, offering enough depth and breadth to hold many layers of meaning. It speaks to us at all stages of our lives, holding interest for both children and adults. It must be simple, yet complex enough to present new insights and illuminations with each hearing. It must be in some sense held communally—shared by a family, a faith community, an ethnic group, or a nation. Often, wisdom tales are stories that have stood the test of time, either as age-old folktales or as the tales of real-life heroes who faced challenges. They are stories that help us answer basic identity questions: Who am I and who are we? Where have we come from? What do we value? What do we know that helps us to respond to the challenges life presents?

Where can such stories be found? Wisdom tales are held communally, so a first question to ask is: What are the beloved stories from your family, community, or congregation? How do they bespeak the understandings of your group? Tales from the wider world—Buddhist Jataka tales, parables, or hero stories—may be especially important to your group. The Unitarian Universalist living tradition calls us to actively seek wisdom and perspectives from many sources. We value wisdom tales from communities other than our own. Engaging with diverse traditions and cultures deepens our understanding of those cultures and of what it means to live well and fully. It can be challenging, though, to bring those tales into our communities in a way that honors and respects both the story and the culture from which it came.

When sharing wisdom tales from a culture and heritage not your own, you are unlikely to perceive the overtones that a story holds for those who have heard and repeated it over a lifetime. In order to understand the story's wisdom and insight, you must learn something of the background of the story and how and why it came to be.

One way to do this is to consult with those whose heritage is of that culture. Members of your faith community, neighborhood, or family may be willing to share from the wealth of wisdom tales they know from their heritage. People from the broader community might also be offered an opportunity to share wisdom tales. If a person is willing to share such tales with your faith community, it is a wonderful gift, one to be honored and respected.

Seek primary cultural and ethnic sources for help. When approaching a story from a group that has been historically marginalized, exploited, or oppressed by the dominant culture, it is crucial to learn about the nature of that exploitation or oppression. Be particularly sensitive when working with stories from Native American/First Nation, African, African American, Asian, or Asian American cultures, if you are not from the same cultural heritage that the tale is from. The overtones perceived by members of a historically marginalized group often involve the ways in which wisdom stories have helped the group maintain its identity in the face of oppression or exploitation. Appreciating the story must include acknowledging this important part of its background. Seeking knowledge about the background and context of a story from an oppressed group is a practice that helps ensure that we treat the gift of those stories with deserved honor and respect. If members of a cultural group urge you not to tell a particular wisdom story at all, then do not.

Wisdom tales from many cultures, traditions, and heritages can be found in published collections, children's literature books, and on the Internet. Look at different published versions of a particular tale, and seek those written or told by members of the group from which the tale originated. If possible, listen to recorded narrations of the story to enable you to better understand its cadences and subtleties, but do not try to use an accent other than your own. Choose a version that conveys meaning in a way that is accessible to listeners. Is there enough detail to allow a listener to imagine the setting and the characters? Is the action simple enough for one from outside the culture to understand what is happening? Is this version complex enough to inspire reflection?

Before telling wisdom tales from a culture or tradition that is not your own, there are key questions to ask. What do we as Unitarian Universalists appreciate or learn from this story? Why are we choosing to include it? How do those who come from this tradition understand and gain from the story and how does that differ from what Unitarian Universalists might understand or gain? How do we do justice to both points of view?

One of the stories I chose to include in this book is from the Anishinabe (Ojibway) tradition. It's a tale about pride, competition, and overreaching that holds wisdom for contemporary people across many cultures. I could identify what wisdom and meaning it held for Unitarian Universalists, but I was not at all clear about the wisdom and meaning the story holds for those of Anishinabe heritage. I did not have a sense of the role Nanabush held in the Anishinabe culture. In fact, I did not know much at all about the role of stories in the culture, nor about the sense of the sacred shared among those of Anishinabe heritage. I needed to learn more before suggesting "Nanabush and the Bulrushes" for this book.

I chose an Anishinabe wisdom tale after reading dozens of First Nation tales. I found myself drawn to the tales from the people of the Great Lakes region, an area I know well because my family has a cottage in the Sault Ste. Marie area of Ontario. For most of my adult life, I have been aware of the Ojibway community living in that area but had never taken the time to learn about that nation. My own position as a member of the dominant culture made it possible for me to be ignorant of a people who lived just a few miles down the road from the family cottage. This ignorance was a painful revelation.

Using the Internet, I quickly learned that many from the culture prefer to call themselves Anishinabe. Scanning scores of websites, I searched particularly for those created and maintained by members of the nation, looking at sections called "Resources" or "For Further Reading." Over time, a list of frequently recommended resources and authors emerged. I sought out those resources and authors, purchasing several books from used books stores in Michigan and Wisconsin.

I read about the history, spirituality, literature, and culture of the Anishinabe and learned of the struggle of leaders to keep the culture and language alive through its sacred stories. I came to know a great deal about the Nanabush—part spirit, part hero, part prototypical human—and the role his stories play in the culture. I read contemporary translations of Anishinabe wisdom literature and commentary on that literature and encountered a book published in 1917 that had Nanabush stories from four different storytellers printed in the Anishinabe language with English translations alongside. In that book, I found two more versions of the story that gave me an even better feel for it.

When I had finally finished rendering the story for this book and suggesting ways in which it can inform and deepen a Unitarian Universalist faith journey, I asked a person of Anishinabe heritage to review my work and to comment. Had I captured the essence of the story? Had biases and assumptions of which I was unaware crept into my telling?

While Unitarian Universalism affirms that there is new revelation to be discovered within our historical, cultural, and religious tradition, we also honor wisdom discovered by other peoples, cultures, and faith traditions. It is wonderfully liberating to draw on multiple perspectives. We are able to perceive our spiritual challenges through a variety of different theological and cultural viewpoints. But there can be risks to our broadly inclusive tradition. We may deny sources the depth of study needed to fully understand the wisdom they have to offer. Taking time to understand something of the cultural context and the background of the stories we tell is necessary to do them justice. When we do this fully and bring our own spiritual challenges to the wisdom stories as well, we grow our spirits and deepen our faith.

It is an honor and a responsibility to be a teller of wisdom stories. Storytelling is an ancient form of teaching, a way of pointing listeners toward deep truths and inviting them to examine their own lives and circumstances. To listen to a story requires suspension of the activities of day-to-day living and entrance into the world of the story. Effectively creating that world for the listener requires that the storyteller prepare to be the carrier of the tale and the wisdom it holds.

When you choose a story to share, your work has just begun. Reflect upon the story and identify why you have chosen it. What in the tale speaks to you? What wisdom resonates with and illuminates your current circumstances? If you have chosen the tale in order to work with a certain theme, think about why you have chosen this story and not some other. How is the wisdom and message of the story consistent with the overall message of the service or lesson? How does the story deepen and enrich that message?

Wisdom stories can be quite complex. Folktale protagonists go on long journeys, encountering adventures and challenges that may be mystifying, or even off-putting, to the modern reader. Snapshots from the biographies of real-life prophets and heroes reveal a hodge-podge of emotions, motivations, and influences surrounding an event, experience, or discovery. Scientific stories of the universe and the earth are anything but simple. Stories from the world's religious traditions grow out of complex cultural and historical contexts. Whether the story is from science or biography, folktale or scripture, the carrier of the story must convey the message simply and effectively. At the same time, the storyteller must include enough complexity to allow the listener to encounter in the story connections with lived experience.

Children's Bibles provide a good illustration. A book that calls itself a children's Bible highlights certain parts of the biblical narrative and tells those stories in ways that convey a particular message deemed appropriate and meaningful for an audience of children. Some children's Bibles simplify the stories, removing ambiguity, complexity, and context. Others provide historical and cultural context for the stories and retain some of their ambiguities and complexities. Each reflects choices made about what to include and what to omit. They reflect the point of view of the author or storyteller.

Published children's books narrating folktales or tales from the world's faith traditions follow the same pattern. The author highlights certain parts of the story and omits or downplays others in order to convey a particular message or experience. A published work cannot include all of the details, plot twists, and subtexts found in the oral and written tradition for a wisdom tale.

To tell a story is to make choices about what content, ambiguity, context, and complexity is appropriate for the intended listener or reader. Whether you are composing a tale from a longer biography of someone's life, from scientific information about the natural world, from scripture, or from longer versions of folktales or religious tales, your task is to make choices that clarify your message.

Reflect on the theological issues in the story and in the message you wish to convey. Questions about the nature of human beings, the origin of the universe, the mystery and nature of life and death, the existence of good and evil, and moral obligations are all theological questions. Most stories reflect one or more of these questions. If a story is nested in a theological point of view that differs from your own, examine the challenge that comes from that different point of view. How does that challenge help you to strengthen and clarify your perspective? Can you convey the wisdom of the tale while maintaining a Unitarian Universalist theological perspective and sensibility?

There are a variety of ways to work with stories that do not perfectly match current Unitarian Universalist theological understandings or sensibilities. One way is to leave theological questions open and ambiguous. The Easter story is a powerful one when told as a story of hope and love triumphing over death and cruelty; the question of resurrection of the body can be left open to interpretation. Another way is to de-emphasize parts of a story that are inconsistent with Unitarian Universalist understandings and dwell on parts that convey wisdom accessible to your listeners and are congruent with current Unitarian Universalist understandings. If you are telling a narrative of a male hero who lived at a time and in a culture when women did not exercise a public voice and presence, you may choose to simply ignore that fact in your telling. It is often important, however, to raise the de-emphasized issue in the conversation following the tale. A third way is to alter nonessential parts of the story to more accurately reflect current Unitarian Universalist sensibilities. In "The Mustard Seed Medicine," a story from the Buddhist tradition, the neighbors that Kisa Gotami visits in search of a mustard seed can live in a variety of different kinds of families. A fourth way of approaching the problem is to offer a brief explanation before beginning that highlights some aspect of the historical, cultural, or theological context of the story.

Once you have clarified the message and decided what to do about the theological and cultural questions and dilemmas raised by the story, it is time to work on the actual telling of the tale. Here, there are still more choices to make. Where and how will the tale begin? Where and how will it end? What are key transition points in the tale? Which scenes deserve carefully painted word images and which can be skimmed over, included merely to advance the plot?

Begin an oral tale simply. Transport your listener quickly to the world of the story. Introduce main characters, the setting, and topic right away; the first few sentences invite your listeners on a journey through a world that you create. End your tale in way that makes it clear to the listener that you have reached the conclusion. You might use formulaic expressions (e.g., "Once upon a time . . ." or "That is the end of my tale") to signal beginnings and endings. Invite listeners to join you in the world of the story and welcome them to make connections with their own lived experience.

How you modulate the middle of a story will determine your degree of success in conveying your message and inviting reflection. Identify one or several peak places in a story where change or transformation is a possibility or a reality. Build your story around those places. Linger, describing scenes, emotions, and reactions to challenges. Focus on your main message, and leave out or downplay inessential characters or details. If these are spots where you need to move the plot along, use wording such as "and so the days (years) passed" or "and she grew up." Repeated words, phrases, or situations can effectively keep the rhythm of the plot moving.

Wisdom stories can be told to intergenerational groups and will be heard differently by people at different stages of life. For the tale to be accessible to all ages, use simple, straightforward language. Not every word must be in the vocabulary of a young child, but the child must be able to grasp the sense of the story from your words, your gestures, your facial expressions, and the way you use your voice to convey meaning. The basic plot and message must be simple enough that a child can follow the story, and even retell it. But you must offer more than just a story for young children, no matter how valuable the message is to their moral and spiritual development. You must offer to those further along in their faith journey a chance for renewal of spirit and recommitment to the values found in the message of the story. Listening together to a wisdom story offers children a chance to feel secure, initiated into the community's story and vision. It offers adults a reaffirmation of that story and vision in their own lives, and the joy of knowing that it is being shared with a new generation. There is power in being together, spellbound by the telling of a story.

Youth and adults wrestle with the same basic moral themes and teachings as those faced by young children: Everyone is important and special, don't take more than your share, be good to other people and the earth, everything is connected and we are part of it, there is always room for hope, and we can work to make things better. But children have less life experience than those further along on life's journey. Adults and youth have learned how hard it can be to honor basic moral teachings. They have memories of times when they have succeeded and times when they have failed. The wisdom story is a reminder of those basic teachings and of our own faith journeys. It offers the opportunity for reflection, for illumination, and for recommitment with each new encounter.

The Unitarian Universalist tradition is held together by a covenant that affirms and promotes certain values and ways of treating one another. That covenant is embodied in our statement of seven Principles. Unitarian Universalism affirms that revelation is neither complete nor sealed. It comes to us from many places. The stories that follow in this volume reflect Unitarian Universalist values, traditions, and wisdom as found in our Principles and Sources.

Each story holds diverse meanings and is intended to be accessible to people of all ages. Each story's particular meaning and wisdom in a Unitarian Universalist context are explored in the supplementary material that follows the story. This material invites you to think about what the story has to teach in terms of three ideas: "Hearing a Calling," "Opening to New Revelation," and "Finding Wisdom Through the Principles and Sources." "Hearing a Calling" refers to understanding the gifts and the contributions that we are called to make to our communities and to the world. "Opening to New Revelation" asks, What insights does this story point to about our own lives and circumstances? And finally, we ask how the story invites us to deeper engagement with the Principles and Sources of our living tradition. Each story is also accompanied by suggested activities and extensions of the story experience for faith communities and for families. May these stories be a starting point for experiences that grow spirits and deepen faith!

# Our Unitarian Universalist Principles

*We, the member congregations of the Unitarian Universalist Association, covenant to affirm and promote:*

The inherent worth and dignity of every person;

Justice, equity and compassion in human relations;

Acceptance of one another and encouragement to spiritual growth in our congregations;

A free and responsible search for truth and meaning;

The right of conscience and the use of the democratic process within our congregations and in society at large;

The goal of world community with peace, liberty and justice for all;

Respect for the interdependent web of all existence of which we are a part.

# The Brementown Musicians

One of the stories collected long ago by Jacob and Wilhelm Grimm, this animal folktale is an account of unlikely friendship and cooperation, in which each animal uses its own skills to help the whole group. It features four animals deemed without value, who go on to find friendship and peace together.

This story invites active listener participation in the process of imaging and creating the tale. Help listeners prepare for its telling by rehearsing sounds for the donkey, dog, cat, and rooster, and by practicing the refrain line, "On the road to Brementown. Musicians they would be," with the group. When reading the story, introduce the animal characters with drama for their tales of woe. With each repeated refrain line, listeners will feel as if they are moving along on the journey. As listeners make noises to indicate the different animals, the story will begin to provide a grand clamor.

A farmer once had a donkey who was growing old and unable to work. Thinking that it was no longer worthwhile to feed the old donkey, the farmer became determined to put an end to him. The donkey sensed that something was amiss, and he ran away, thinking that he would go to Bremen and become a musician. He was:

On the road to Brementown.
A musician he would be.

After he had traveled a way, the donkey came upon a tired dog lying beside the road and panting. "What are you doing lying there, my friend?" he asked.

"Alas, I am old and weak and can no longer hunt, so my master decided to do away with me. I ran away, but now I don't know how to make my living. The only thing I can still do is bark."

"Well," said the donkey, "you and your bark can join me. I'm off to become a town musician in Bremen." And when the dog joined him, they were:

> On the road to Brementown.
> Musicians they would be.

It was not long before they came upon a cat sitting in the road, looking mournful. "What's the matter with you?" said the donkey. "Why are you looking so sad?"

"Oh," meowed the cat. "How can I be cheerful when my life is in danger? I am growing old and would rather lie about by the fire than chase mice, so my mistress resolved to drown me. I ran away from her, but I don't know what I shall do to earn my food."

"Well," said the donkey, "you are certainly a good singer! Come and join us. We're going to Bremen to become town musicians." The cat quickly agreed, and they were:

> On the road to Brementown.
> Musicians they would be.

Soon enough, they came upon a rooster perched on a farm-yard gate, screaming for all he was worth. "Cock-a-doodle-doo! Woe is me! Tomorrow they will put me in the soup pot. Whatever am I to do?"

"You can certainly add something to a concert," said the donkey. He invited the rooster to join the group. In short order, they were:

> On the road to Brementown.
> Musicians they would be.

The animals could not reach the town in one day, so they decided to settle in the forest for the night. The donkey and dog lay under a tree, and the cat in the branches. The rooster flew to the topmost branch and had a look around. "There must be a house not a far way off," said the rooster, "for I can see a small light."

Hungry and cold, all four agreed to go and see if they might find food and shelter. When they arrived at the cabin, they arranged themselves to peek in the window. The donkey put his front paws against the side of the cabin; the dog climbed on his back. The cat sat on the dog's shoulders and the rooster flew up to sit on the cat's head. When he looked inside, the rooster reported seeing some robbers sitting and making merry in front of the fire. There was a table spread with all manner of good food.

The foursome made a plan for getting rid of the robbers. At the donkey's signal, all four of the Brementown musicians began to sing. The donkey brayed, the dog barked, the cat meowed, and the rooster screamed. The frightened robbers ran from the place, leaving the wonderful feast to the four friends, who happily ate their fill and settled down to sleep.

After a time, the most courageous of the robbers decided to come back. All was quiet, and he thought perhaps they had left too hastily. He made his way cautiously into the dark cabin. He saw the cat's eyes, looking like two live coals. He took out a match to strike, and the cat sprang at his face and scratched him. He ran for the back door, but the dog jumped up and bit him in the leg. As he crossed the yard, the donkey kicked him, and all the while the rooster screamed, "Cock a-doodle-doo!"

The robber made his way back to his companions and hastily told of his encounters in the cabin: "A horrid witch scratched me with her bony fingers, then a man with a knife stabbed me, a monster with a club beat me, and the devil sat on top of the cabin crying all the while calling, 'Bring the rascal here!'"

The robbers never dared to go back to the cabin again, and the four friends remain together to this day, making music in the woods.

## Meaning and Wisdom for Unitarian Universalists

*Hearing a Calling*
This is a tale of discarded animal characters deemed no longer use-ful. Sensing impending doom, each of them has run away. They are in search but are unsure what they are searching for. Each finds a new sense of purpose when invited to be part of a group of friends. They become the Brementown musicians and their identities are made secure. They matter to the group; they belong.

The story reminds us that we need others to help us to get back on track, others who call us to make our unique contribution to the whole. We find purpose joining one another in making the joyful music of life.

*Opening to New Revelation*
Underneath all the noise and fun of this story, there are some dark themes. The four animal characters are each in trouble because their masters or owners decided that they are no longer worth-while or useful. The owners are narrowly defining what gifts are useful in each being. In our own society, we wrestle with difficult ethical questions about the value of each life. Debates rage about whether the cost to educate or care for a child or adult with signifi-cant disabilities is worth it. Lawmakers make budgetary decisions about how much money will go to fund homeless shelters or drug and alcohol treatment programs. What insight and wisdom does this tale offer as we engage the thorny ethical questions of our day? There is revelation here for children and adults alike.

*Finding Wisdom Through the Principles and Sources*
This story is a wonderful, fun reminder of our first Principle, which affirms the inherent worth and dignity of every person. Four ani-mal characters are discarded for having outlived their usefulness, but they find new life with companions who value them and cel-ebrate their uniqueness. Each is able to make a contribution to the group. And the song they sing together is just the right one to sing.

## Connecting with Our Lives

*In Our Faith Communities*
This story is ideal for a celebration of friendship, either as part of a worship service or as a special event. Children can practice with a storyteller and present it to the congregation, complete with sound effects. When talking with children about the story, encourage them to name one way in which they contribute their unique "songs" to life. What does each person bring that is appreciated by others? What qualities do we value in friends? What do we offer of ourselves to our friends?

"The Brementown Musicians" is an old tale that has wisdom to offer in our own world. Engage youth or adults in conversation about those who are "discarded" as not worthy, those who are homeless or mentally ill or poor, or who have difficulty fitting in. How do the animal characters feel about being deemed useless? How do they respond? What do our faith tradition and our Principles tell us about those whom society discards? Are there ways that the congregation puts the first Unitarian Universalist Principle of affirming the worth and dignity of all into action?

*At Home*
With young children, this story can be a fun celebration of the ways in which we support one another and work together. Engage your family in a project that requires cooperation and a contribution from each member: Planting a garden, cooking a meal, constructing a stone wall, making a snowman, or building a sand castle are some ideas. Talk with children about what it means to be part of a group such as a family, neighborhood, school class, or congregation. In what ways does each person make an individual contribution to the work and play of the group?

Older children and teens can use the story as a springboard for conversation about how society discards or deems unworthy certain kinds of people. What wisdom do Unitarian Universalist faith and Principles offer us? How can we work to assure that every person is valued? Visiting those who live in nursing homes, working to end homelessness or hunger, and inviting someone without family close by to a family holiday celebration are just some of the ways to affirm the worth and dignity of every person.

# Creation

This story is based on the first of two versions of the creation story found in chapters 1 and 2 of the Book of Genesis in the Hebrew Bible. In this version, man and woman are created together, both in the image of God. The seven-day creation story, while not scientifically accurate, contains ancient wisdom. It is a hymn of praise to all of creation, poetry that names and lingers over all the wonders of the world. It is presented here as a reading in two voices: a "Bible voice" that is the text itself, and an "appreciating voice" that lingers in gratitude and praise over the wonders enumerated in the text.

In this well-known passage of scripture, God "talks the world into being." His or her actions bring order out of chaos. He or she divides, differentiates, and categorizes, bringing about the order of night and day, sea and sky, plants and animals. By naming things God identifies each as separate and different from one another. In turn each is given meaning. The God of Genesis blesses each creature. This gesture acknowledges, rather than confers, the sacredness of all living things. It invites us also to name and bless all of the wonders of our world.

APPRECIATING VOICE: Sometimes, when I look up at the stars, or feel the rain on my face, or hear the buzzing of a bee, I wonder where it all came from. How did we begin? I know the wisdom that comes from science, which says that microscopic one-celled creatures evolved over millions of years into countless compli-

cated forms of life. But sometimes, when I behold the wonder
of it all, I love to hear the words spoken long ago by the ancient
Hebrews about how the earth and the sky and all things living were
called into being and blessed by the Spirit of Life we sometimes
call God.

BIBLE VOICE: In the beginning, when God created the heavens and
the earth, the earth was a formless void and darkness. A wind from
God swept over the face of the waters. Then God said, "Let there
be light," and there was light. God called the light Day, and the
darkness Night. And there was evening and there was morning the
first day.

APPRECIATING VOICE: From the beginning, light and darkness,
activity and rest, day and night.

BIBLE VOICE: And God said, "Let there be a dome in the midst of
the waters, and let it separate the waters from the waters." God
called the dome Sky. And there was evening and there was morning, the second day.

APPRECIATING VOICE: From the mountaintop, the treetop, the air-
plane, or our own backyards, we see the daytime clouds and nighttime stars that reach further than we can even imagine. From the
canoe, the rocky bluff or the sandy shore, we see the vastness of the
sea, deeper and wider than we can fully understand. In the presence of sky or of sea, we feel connected to the mystery of life.

BIBLE VOICE: And God said, "Let the waters under the sky be gathered together into one place and let the dry land appear." And it was
so. God called the dry land Earth, and the waters that were called
together Seas. And God saw that it was good. Then God said, "Let
the earth put forth vegetation: plants yielding seed, and fruit trees
of every kind on earth that bear fruit with the seed in it." And it was
so. And there was evening and there was morning, the third day.

APPRECIATING VOICE: Chestnuts, acorns, dandelions, and beans—each carries the beginning of a brand-new plant. We plant apple seeds and peach pits, wheat, peas, and corn. We watch day by day for the avocado seed in a glass to sprout or the bean to split and put down roots. We are grateful for the plants and the trees that bring us beauty, joy, and good food—and for those plants that protect themselves with thorns, poison leaves, and tall, winding branches.

BIBLE VOICE: And God said, "Let there be lights in the dome of the sky to separate the day from the night; and let them be for signs and for seasons and for days and years." God made the two great lights—the greater light to rule the day and the lesser light to rule the night—and the stars. And there was evening, and there was morning, the fourth day.

APPRECIATING VOICE: We give thanks for the orbit of our earth around its sun. It brings the seasons: times for planting and for harvest, time to enjoy the warmth of the sun, and time to pull closer to the fire for warmth. We give thanks also for our earth's moon, which causes the tidal coming and going of the oceans.

BIBLE VOICE: And God said, "Let the waters bring forth swarms of living creatures, and let birds fly above the earth across the dome of the sky." So God created the great sea monsters and every living creature that moves, of every kind, with which the waters swarm, and every winged bird of every kind. And God saw that it was good. God blessed them, saying, "Be fruitful and multiply and fill the waters in the seas, and let the birds multiply on the earth." And there was evening and there was morning, the fifth day.

APPRECIATING VOICE: Blessing all the creatures of the earth, the sea, and the sky, God acknowledged that each is sacred.

BIBLE VOICE: And God said, "Let the earth bring forth living creatures of every kind: cattle and creeping things and wild animals, and everything that creeps upon the ground." And God saw that it was good.

Then God said, "Let us make humankind in our image."
So God created humankind in his image,
In the image of God he created them
Male and female he created them.

God blessed them and said, "Be fruitful and multiply and fill the earth."

And there was evening, and there was morning, the sixth day.

APPRECIATING VOICE: We, too, can bless the animals of every kind on the face of the earth. We can recognize the divine, the Creative Spirit, the Spirit of Life in each of them and in each of us. We rejoice in the blessing of being alive and sharing the gift of life with the creatures of this, our planet home.

BIBLE VOICE: Thus the heavens and the earth were finished, and all their multitude. And on the seventh day God finished the work. And on that day God rested. So God blessed the seventh day.

## Meaning and Wisdom for Unitarian Universalists

### Hearing a Calling
To name something or someone is to acknowledge its separate and distinct existence. When we dedicate and name a child, we are affirming that that child is a separate being and acknowledging even a young person's innate sacredness. Unitarian Universalism is a faith for seekers. Searching, seeing, and naming are faithful acts. We are called to see and name our individual sacred truths.

### Opening to New Revelation
The Genesis creation story reminds us of the presence of mystery and sacredness in our lives. Noticing and naming can be powerful

acts for Unitarian Universalists. Looking with great attention at the world around us nurtures a theology of gratitude and places us at the threshold of new revelations.

*Finding Wisdom Through the Principles and Sources*
Creation unfolds in ever more diverse and complex forms. The tendency of the world, even centuries ago, was toward ever increasing diversity in the life that fills the seas, the sky, and the land.

Unitarian Universalists, in celebrating diversity of experience, of understanding, and of perspective are mirroring creation itself in its drive toward diverse forms of life.

## Connecting with Our Lives

*In Our Faith Communities*
Children may ask if the creation story found in Genesis and re-told here is true. You can invite them to think about times long ago, when tools of science were few. Ancient Hebrews understood things in their own way, often relying on their observations as their only tools. For example, on the second day, God creates a dome called sky and on the fourth day, puts the sun and moon in the dome as lights. Nowadays, we know that the sky is not a closed dome. We know that our earth revolves around the sun, and not the other way around. But we still can still experience the sky the way the ancients did, wondering at the beauty of the sun, moon, and stars from our own particular place on earth.

Children can learn to claim the word *blessing* as a way of ac-knowledging sacredness. Take children to their favorite outdoor spot and bless the living things you find there. In faith education settings, offering a blessing before snacks or meals affirms the sacred mystery of our own bodies, nourished by the essence of other sacred beings, plants and animals.

*At Home*

Naming can be a powerful act. Talk with family members about their names and the endearments they use for each other. Adults and children may wish to investigate the meanings of their own names. Help children remember names they assigned to special people or things as they were growing up. Talk about how naming acknowledges a relationship between the people who name and are named. We seek these connections just as the Hebrew people did years ago. And that, too, forges connections between generations and between faith traditions, ancient and new.

# Jack and the Northwest Wind

Wisdom stories can journey through time and cultures. The universal appeal of such stories attests to the shared human terrain of our diverse life journeys. This story comes from the oral folk tradition of Appalachia and features a character named Jack, who is central to many Appalachian folktales. Jack tales usually involve a young man who is searching for a solution to a problem that is troubling his home community. Like all of us, Jack wants to help make things better. And like all of us, he is often imperfect in his quest. Most of the tales about Jack are adaptations of stories from Northern Europe that have been altered to meet the needs and sensibilities of the rural Appalachian culture.

Tracing a Jack tale's evolution can be akin to tracing the life journeys of family members who keep changing their names. This story, "Jack and the Northwest Wind," seems to be a variant of "The Table, the Ass, and the Stick," a story first recorded by Jacob and Wilhelm Grimm. This version was recorded in 1943 by Richard Chase, who collected tales told by others. There are more recent versions in many current story collections as well.

A major hallmark of the Jack tales, including this one, is a strong sense of community and place. The Appalachian Jack is a young man who grows out of his rural community and always returns to it. In this story, Jack ventures out in the world in order to stop the winter wind, which is making him cold. Along the way, he receives magical help, and a good dose of advice, from a wise stranger. He encounters problems and makes mistakes, but in the long run, he triumphs. Through it all, both the wise man and Jack's mother not only support and encourage his adventuring but also refrain from anger and harsh judgment when he gets into trouble. Listeners, however, often wonder if this will indeed be the case.

The winter wind blew and blew at the top of the mountain, where Jack and his mother lived in a drafty little cabin. It blew so hard that they couldn't stay warm no matter how much wood they put on the fire. One day, Jack decided that he had had enough of the wind and enough of the cold.

"I'm going to go and find where that northwest wind begins and I'm going to plug up that hole with my raggedy old cap."

"Be careful, Jack," his mother said. "You never know who you'll meet or what you'll find along the way."

And off he went, looking for the place where the wind begins. Jack had traveled quite a way and was getting pretty hungry when he met an old man.

"Where are you going?"

"I'm going to where the wind begins and I'm going to plug that hole with my raggedy old cap."

"You have a long search ahead of you to find such a place. Surely you must be hungry! Come on into my cabin. I'll give you something to help you on your way."

Into the old man's cabin they went, and the man took out an old tablecloth. He put it on the table and said, "Spread, tablecloth, spread."

At once there appeared a meal with all of Jack's favorite foods: corn, beans, stewed chicken, and apple pie. A hungry Jack ate until he could eat no more. When he thanked the old man and turned to leave, the man folded the cloth and gave it to him, along with a warning: "Be careful of the rowdy boys who live down the road. They are up to no good!"

Sure enough, a short time after he left the old man's cabin, Jack met up with the rowdy boys.

"Where are you going?"

"I'm going to where the wind begins and I'm going to plug that hole with my raggedy old cap."

"So what have you got there?"

After they pestered him for a while, Jack couldn't resist showing the boys his cloth. "Spread, tablecloth, spread!" he commanded. And the tablecloth was filled with delicious food.

The rowdy boys began to plot to steal the cloth. They invited Jack to stay the night in their warm cabin. While he slept, they took his magic cloth and left him a plain old tablecloth.

The next day, when Jack awoke, he decided to take the cloth home to his mother. He was eager to show her what he had been given. His mother watched as he spread it out and commanded, "Spread, tablecloth, spread!" But nothing happened.

"That's okay, Jack," said his mother. "I'm just glad you are home." And she showed him how to make a shirt from the cloth.

It wasn't long before the northwest wind began to blow again through the walls of their cabin, and Jack set out once more to find where the wind begins and plug the hole.

Once again, he met the old man on the path. Jack told the old man that the cloth didn't work anymore. "Did you stop and talk with those rowdy boys I warned you about?" When Jack admitted that he had shown the cloth to the boys, the old man shook his head.

"You are a good boy, though," said the old man, "and I'm going to give you something else to help you out." He picked up a hen from the corner by the fireplace. "Hold your cap under the hen, Jack." Then the old man commanded, "Come, golden egg, come!"

In Jack's cap lay a golden egg. "You take this hen home to your mama," said the man, "and be sure to stay away from those rowdy boys."

Jack started out with the hen under his arm. And it wasn't long before he once again met up with the rowdy boys.

"What's the hen for?" they asked.

"It's for my mama," said Jack. When the boys began to tease Jack about carrying around a hen, he couldn't resist showing them how the hen laid a golden egg. And it wasn't long before the rowdy boys had tricked Jack again, keeping his hen and giving him an ordinary one instead.

Once again, Jack went home with something special for his mother. But when he commanded the hen to lay, nothing happened. "That's okay, Jack," she said. "I'm glad you are home safe, and thankful to have something for dinner." And with that, she cooked the hen and they enjoyed it together.

But it wasn't long before the northwest wind blew again through the walls of their cabin. Jack set out one more time. For a third time, he met the old man on the path. "Jack, where are you going?"

"I'm going to where the wind begins and I'm going to plug that hole with my raggedy old cap."

"I gave you a hen that laid golden eggs so you could buy wood and a hammer and fix up the holes in your cabin. What happened?"

And Jack told him about meeting the rowdy boys and how they had tricked him and stolen the hen.

The old man said, "If you will promise to go right back home and forget about looking for the beginning of the wind, I'll give you one last gift." And the old man took Jack into his cabin and took out a big, knotty stick. "You'll need to be careful with this and stay away from those boys." And he said to the stick, "Play away, club, play away."

And the stick flew out of his hand and began to knock down trees, chop them for firewood, and stack it on the porch. "It will chop and chop until you tell it, 'Stop, stick, stop!' Take it home with you—and be careful of the rowdy boys!"

Jack headed toward home, but it wasn't long before he met the rowdy boys once again. They talked him into showing what the stick would do. When they saw it chopping and stacking wood, they were amazed, and began to plot about stealing this, too. Jack agreed to spend the night but insisted that he would sleep with the stick in his hand.

One of the boys came in while Jack slept and took the stick out of his hands. "Play away, club, play away!" the boy said. And the stick began to move rapidly back and forth. It knocked down and chopped all the furniture in the whole house! Jack woke up and said, "This stick will take down your walls and your roof and your whole house unless you give back my hen and my tablecloth." Frightened, the boys gave Jack back his tablecloth and his hen. "Stop, stick, stop!" commanded Jack. Smiling, he gathered up his three magical gifts and went home.

From then on, he and his mother had enough food to eat, enough money to repair their cabin, and firewood to keep them warm when the winter winds blew.

Jack never again looked for the place where the wind begins.

## Meaning and Wisdom for Unitarian Universalists

*Hearing a Calling*

No matter what has happened and how many mistakes he has made, Jack is always able to go home and prepare himself for the next chapter of his life's journey. Over and over, Jack is called to try again. Even when he fails to reach his intended destination and when he allows himself to be tricked by the rowdy boys, he remains undeterred. He tries again to solve the problem of the wind in his home. He is called to help and his persistence throughout the tale makes that more and more clear.

Welcomed back after every mistake, Jack's sense of connection to his home is repeatedly affirmed. When he finally gets the better of the rowdy boys and retrieves his magical objects, Jack has clearly learned from his experiences. His rewards are not what he expected; they surpass what he was originally seeking. We connect to Jack's persistence in this story and to his calling to help his family home. The quest becomes more clearly a quest of the heart.

### Opening to New Revelation

Jack's simple task becomes complicated in this tale. He is forced to shift his focus from learning how to block the wind in his home to learning how to help his family home more broadly. Sometimes Jack is able to learn from his experiences, but he is unable to summon that new knowledge until the close of the story. He simply doesn't seem ready to have and act on his knowledge of the rowdy boys until the time is right. Like all seekers, Jack must be ready to embody what he has learned. Sometimes we, like Jack, must let go of a lens that obstructs our new vision. We may be willing to be open to new revelation, but sometimes we need to wait for life's unfolding to find it.

### Finding Wisdom Through the Principles and Sources

This folktale invites us to consider our third Unitarian Universalist Principle, acceptance of one another and encouragement to spiritual growth. Jack finds that home offers him both acceptance and encouragement to learn and to grow. He is always able to go home. Jack's mother meets his failings and turns disappointments into positives. He is always given another chance. When he finally gets the better of the rowdy boys and retrieves his magical objects, Jack has clearly learned from his experiences.

On his adventures, Jack is presented with three magical objects, unearned treasures to help him along his way. There are for each of us unearned treasures that enrich our lives, and it is up to us to use those treasures to help us grow in spirit. Jack's generosity and commitment to his family make him worthy of the three objects.

## Connecting with Our Lives

### In Our Faith Communities

Children will respond to different aspects of this tale. Invite them to explore different themes. One provocative aspect of this story is Jack's encounters with the rowdy boys. While we might wish for a magic club to scare away bullies, such items don't exist outside of our story. What are some ways children and adults can stand up for themselves with bullies? How might people keep from being talked into doing something they know to be unwise? Engage in authentic conversation. When adults are willing to share some of their own experiences, it encourages children to do the same.

Jack is given three magical objects and they do very specific things. There is a tablecloth that keeps him and his mother from going hungry; a hen that lays a golden egg that allows them to buy a hammer, boards, and nails to fix the cabin; and a stick that chops their firewood. They do not use the golden eggs from the hen to become fabulously wealthy but only to give them what they need to make them comfortable and content. What kind of magical object would children like to receive? If their magical object gives them gold or money, what would they want to do with it? Children can be invited to work separately or together on a clay model, a collage, or a painting of their magical object, and then share it with others.

*At Home*

"Jack and the Northwest Wind" provides a good basis for family discussion. What makes this tale so easy for children to enjoy is that, despite his failings, Jack triumphs in the end. He makes mistakes and learns from them. Being forgiven, loved, and supported is part of being a family. Invite children to share incidents when they felt welcome in their family even when they had made a mistake or forgotten something important. Engage children in stories of family mistakes. Remember times when following advice has lead to happy endings; remember times when advice ignored similarly turned out well.

# The Lion's Whisker

Loving friendships and family relationships take time. This story is about a young woman who wants very badly to be a good stepmother but needs some help to learn how to establish trust and love with her new stepson. A healer guides her and she discovers that all that she needs to establish the mother–son relationship is already within her.

This story has many versions, both in Ethiopia and in Korea. It speaks to a universal truth about families, that good relationships require tending. Trust cannot be forced, nor can it be bought with gifts. Loving relationships require patience, time, and deliberate attention. The woman in this tale from long ago seeks quick change, a magic potion to make her stepson love her. Instead, the wise healer offers her a journey. The answer she seeks lies up the mountain outside the lion's den—and inside her own spirit.

Once upon a time there was a young woman who was a brand-new wife and a brand-new stepmother to her husband's son. Her husband's first wife, the boy's mother, had died some years earlier and left both father and son lonely and sad. The new wife wanted nothing more keenly than to be a good stepmother to the boy, one who would share happy times and sad ones, see to his needs, and help him to grow up wise and strong.

But, alas, things were not as she had hoped. The boy wanted

absolutely nothing to do with his new stepmother. He spoke crossly
to her no matter what she offered him. He reminded her time and
time again that she was not his real mother. The woman spent
many hours weeping over her stepson's rejection, which distressed
her husband greatly.

One day, the woman decided that things could not continue
as they were. Desperate for help, she visited the village healer. She
poured out a tale of her sadness, of her efforts to win over her
stepson, and of how unfairly he treated her in return. She asked the
healer to provide a potion that would make her stepson love her
as a mother. The healer felt great compassion for the woman and
offered to help on one condition. "Before I can help you, you must
find a ferocious lion and bring me one of its whiskers."

The woman had no idea how to fulfill this challenge, but she
was determined to find the special ingredient for the potion. She
went home and packed some fresh meat, and slowly climbed the
mountain to find the lion's den. As she climbed, she heard the lion
roaring in the distance, farther up the mountain, and she walked
toward the sound. When the roar sounded very close by, she left
the fresh meat in a clearing and crouched some distance away in
the bushes to watch. The lion came upon the meat and sniffed the
air before eating. He surely smelled the presence of the woman,
but the meat was attractive. He hungrily gobbled it down.

The next morning, the woman packed another piece of meat.
This time, she knew her way to the lion's den. She found the lion
asleep, more or less, and she tiptoed over to place the meat near
his feet. She withdrew to the bushes, but not quite so far away as
the day before. When the lion awoke, he spied the meat. He sniffed
the air again and surely knew of the woman's presence as he ate the
meat provided for him.

On the third day, the lion was wide-awake when the woman
returned. She showed herself and he seemed to recognize her. The
woman greeted the lion as she took out meat and placed it in front
of him. He ate rather slowly, eyeing her all the while. After a time,
he let her approach and run her hands through his mane.

Thus the days passed. Each day, the woman climbed the mountain and brought meat for the lion. She learned how to approach the lion and how he liked to be patted. She even sang to the lion, which seemed to soothe him. At long last, the right day came for the woman to ask for the lion's whisker. Seeming to understand her need, the lion turned his face toward the woman. She gently plucked a whisker from his chin.

Carefully carrying the lion's whisker, the woman returned to the healer. "Here it is," she said. "Now will you make that potion so that my stepson will love me?"

The healer looked at her kindly and said, "You have made friends with the lion. It took great patience and compassion to do that. You must use the patience that you have learned in order to make friends with your stepson. You don't need a potion. You know deep inside yourself what must be done."

So the woman went home and treated her stepson even better than she had treated the lion, approaching him quietly and with great compassion and patience. In time, he learned to love and trust her, and she learned how to be the best stepmother a boy could ever wish to have.

## Meaning and Wisdom for Unitarian Universalists

*Hearing a Calling*
We do not always take the time necessary to nurture and support our family relationships. We can be quick to blame those we love for not responding to us as we would like them to. This story calls us to look inside ourselves for qualities that heal and nurture relationships: patience, kindness, and a willingness to truly notice and appreciate others. It affirms that these qualities are present in all of us.

## Opening to New Revelation

This story is a journey of discovery. Distraught about her troubled relationship with her stepson, the woman seeks a magic potion to change him. The healer offers, instead, a journey that changes her; her search for the lion's whisker helps her to discover in herself patience, creativity, and compassion. The solution that she seeks from the healer is delivered in an unexpected form as the healer helps her to understand the wisdom of bringing the same attention to her relationship with her stepson that she brought to her encounter with the lion.

## Finding Wisdom Through the Principles and Sources

In "The Lion's Whisker," the search for truth and meaning takes a young woman in unexpected directions. We are reminded that a free and responsible search can, and often will, lead us in different and unanticipated directions. During our search what we are gaining is not always clear. Unitarian Universalism affirms that meaning comes through the process of search; embarking on our life's journeys is a soulful pursuit.

## Connecting with Our Lives

### In Our Faith Communities

The stepmother's situation may feel familiar to many families in congregations. Our individual yearnings for more loving relationships are unspoken common ground. There might also be blended families in your faith community. You may wish to share this story with those families prior to sharing it with children. Invite parents into conversation about it; be especially sensitive to their needs and concerns. Point out to children that this is the story of a kind stepmother, one that balances the wicked stepmother stories they have heard in fairy tales.

This is a story that lends itself to puppet theater. Although it has few characters, two or three children can work on each puppet together. Depending on the age of the children, create simple

paper bag or sock puppets or use more complicated media to create the lion, the woman, the healer, and her husband and son.

This story provides an opening to talk with children about
our fourth Unitarian Universalist Principle, the search for truth
and meaning. Invite children to imagine what advice the healer
might give to other people with different problems. How might
the healer launch them on journeys of self-discovery? Role-play
some conversations between the very wise healer and others who
might have come to the healer. Children can pretend to come to
the healer looking for a potion to solve a family problem or a problem with friends. The entire group can help the healer invent a
wise solution to the problem to be offered instead of a potion.

### At Home

This story offers the opportunity for families to share their own
stories about family struggles or misunderstandings. Has time ever
been part of solving a family problem? If there had been a magic
potion to help clear things up, what would have been in it? How
have family members served as healers to each other? Sometimes
simply pointing out problem-solving capacities or kindness in
others is all that is needed.

Sometimes families create routines and patterns that evolve
over time. If there is a family pet, there are usually stories to retell
about how the pet grew accustomed to the family. Look through
old pictures or other mementoes of times spent with the family,
noticing how patience, kindness, time, and attention helped a pet
to become a member of the family.

# King of the Birds

Tales like this one are part of the folklore of many different cultures. There are references to its appearance in a Jewish collection from the thirteenth century; there are variants in Irish, Scottish, Manx, English, Dutch, Danish, and Norwegian folk cultures. Jacob and Wilhelm Grimm published a version in *German Household Tales* in 1812. Similar stories appear in both Chippewa and Ojibway folklore in North America and in a tale from India. Often the "King of the Birds" tales are written as explanations for why a particular kind of small bird darts about noisily.

Each version of the tale has its own natural setting; the trees, the terrain, and the kinds of birds are drawn from the familiar surroundings of the storyteller. A surprising and wonderful version of the tale was collected and translated by Loreen McDonald, a first-grade teacher at the John Wesley School in Eshowe, Zululand, Natal, South Africa. The tale that follows draws from this Zulu version, which portrays the birds deciding together who will be their leader—with an unexpected result.

Once upon a time, when the world was new, the Great Eagle called a meeting of all the birds. On a bright beautiful morning, they all assembled: the flamingo, the weaver, the steppe buzzard, the warbler, the owl, and all the other birds of the wild.

There was chirping, hooting, and all manner of singing as

the assembled birds greeted one another. Eagle called for silence. When all had quieted down, he said, "We know that Lion is king of all who dwell on the land. But a land dweller like Lion should not rule the birds of the air. We must choose our own leader!" There was great cawing and chirping and chattering of agreement. When all was quiet again, Eagle spoke once more: "The King of Birds should behave like a king. I am the bird with royal bearing. I am the best choice for king!"

The birds murmured and mumbled.

Another voice spoke: "Yes, you are indeed majestic. But I think I, Owl, should be king. I have the largest eyes of any of you and can see everything that happens. I am known for my wisdom and will know best how to act when the king must choose wisely."

The birds began to chatter and argue back and forth. Should their leader have wisdom like Owl or majesty like Eagle? Or perhaps strength like that of the steppe buzzard was the most important thing. The birds had chosen sides and were preparing to vote on who should be their king when another voice emerged from the chatter. It was the voice of the tiny warbler: "I'd like to be king. I think you should elect me!"

The assembled birds began to laugh. What a silly idea! Electing this small warbler king was unthinkable! How dare this ridiculous little bird even suggest such a thing! "Whatever makes you think we should consider choosing a bird like you for our leader? What have you got to offer? You are not the wisest, or the strongest, or the most majestic of the birds," said Eagle.

"Well," said Warbler, "I think I'm as able to be a good king as any of you others who have declared yourselves. I want the opportunity to try!"

The birds laughed. "He certainly has courage," one said.

"Let's have a contest!" declared Eagle, and every bird agreed. "We will meet right after the next full moon. We'll wait until the sun is going down, and when it touches the very top of the mountain, the contest will begin. We'll all fly as high as we can go, maybe even high enough to touch the place where the sky begins. Whoever flies highest will be our new king."

When the contest day arrived, all the birds met once more. Warbler was among the birds who gathered. He had figured out a special plan to prove that he had as much right to be king as any other bird. Just before the beginning of the contest, Warbler crept under Eagle's wing. He pushed his way so deep into Eagle's feathers that as Eagle flew upward, determined to win the contest, he did not feel Warbler buried deep in his feathers.

The birds flew higher and higher. The ones with small wings were soon out of the competition, unable to soar with the larger birds. In time, there were only three birds remaining: Eagle, Owl, and Buzzard. They were exhausted, but they pushed on, flying ever higher. When Owl could no longer continue, he dove back toward earth, resigned. Up and up, higher and higher flew Eagle and Buzzard, until at long last even Buzzard gave up, too exhausted to continue. When Eagle saw that Buzzard was not able to continue, he flew just a little higher and proudly declared himself the contest winner—and the new King of the Birds!

"Not so fast," chirped Warbler, who emerged from Eagle's feathers. "You have not won yet!" And Warbler rose above Eagle, who could not muster the strength to continue flying.

The birds did not declare Warbler their king. They were angered by his trickery and ready to pounce upon him when he came back down. Warbler was frightened by their anger and flew into a deserted snake hole, where he hid from all the others. Owl was appointed to watch the entrance to the hole night and day, lest the little bird escape without facing the consequences of his trickery.

After a while, Owl grew tired. He decided to close one eye and watch with the other. It wasn't long after that when his second eye closed as well and Owl fell asleep. Warbler, who had been waiting for this moment, flew out of the hole and deep into the forest, where even today he flits from place to place, never staying long enough to be caught, calling "I am king! I am king!"

And to this day the birds are still undecided about who should be king.

## Meaning and Wisdom for Unitarian Universalists

### Hearing a Calling

The tiny warbler is called to leadership in this story, as are Owl and Eagle. Warbler thinks that he deserves as much chance as anyone else to be a leader. For him, his size does not matter. It takes courage for Warbler to challenge the other birds. Acting on his own sense of fairness, Warbler is faithful to what he thinks is just. He engages in trickery, but to him the contest itself possesses trickery, since it puts some birds at an advantage over others.

### Opening to New Revelation

The contest is designed to favor candidates who are physically the strongest. Warbler decides to circumvent a system that is already unfair. But instead of focusing on the unjust aspects of the contest, Warbler's peers concentrate on his unfair action. They are not open to thinking about the structure of the contest; they think only about the contestants. Being open to new ideas can involve reconsidering structures that we assume are natural or the way things always are. Thinking through that which we are used to can lead us to new understandings.

### Finding Wisdom Through the Principles and Sources

The fifth Unitarian Universalist Principle affirms the use of the democratic process. Part of our democratic process involves selecting those to whom we entrust leadership. How are those decisions made? Is the person who sees everything and is therefore wise the person we choose as a leader? Is the person with majestic bearing, charisma, or the ability to conduct a public meeting the one we choose as a leader? Do we fail to be open to those who might bring other valuable qualities, skills, and experiences? Are we open to new visions of leadership?

This simple story can spark conversation about the qualities we seek in congregational and in political leaders.

## Connecting with Our Lives

### In Our Faith Communities

Children and families might enjoy transplanting this tale to their own culture, identifying birds, trees, and terrain that are common to their area. Which local birds will play the role of Eagle? Owl? Buzzard? Warbler? Use a bird identification book to find out about the various birds of your area, or invite an expert. Turn this story into a short play with children. Invite them to create a distinct voice for the birds they are playing.

Reflect with children upon Warbler's trickery. In using his cunning to defeat the bigger birds, is he cheating? What about the contest itself? Is it fair to all the birds? Is it a good way to select a leader? What might be a better way to select a leader? Invite children to invent a different kind of contest to determine a leader, and act it out. Older children or youth can examine our public election process and reflect upon whether those contests are weighted toward particular kinds of people.

### At Home

Are leaders always necessary? Talk with children about leadership in your home. Do different people lead in different realms? In this story all the leader contestants are male. Does gender matter for leadership? Does it matter in your family? Help children broaden their ideas of leadership. Sometimes leaders do not fly the highest or stand in the front. The greatest leaders sometimes play the role of gently supporting others.

# Orfeo and Heurodis

This is a "happily-ever-after" love story, a real fairy tale with a king and queen, knights, an enchanted tree, a Fairy King, and magic. The story blends the ancient Greek Orpheus and Eurydice myth with a traditional English fairy tale. In it the hero's journey leads him to use his musical gift, rather than a sword, to solve a problem. It is a story about creativity and the power of music to touch our souls.

Have fun with this story. Invite listeners to describe the fairies and their delightful land as you set the story's stage. Linger over the time Orfeo spends in the forest in despair, playing music for his lost love and captivating the woodland animals. Rejoice with your listeners at the reunion of knight and queen. Imagine music so beautiful that it could enchant a Fairy King. When sharing the story with a group, enlist the help of a harpist to add a musical dimension to your telling.

Once upon a time there was a king called Orfeo who loved Heurodis, his queen, very much. One summer afternoon, Heurodis went walking in the apple orchard. The warm afternoon made her drowsy and she fell asleep under the branches of an imp tree.

Heurodis had a strange dream while she was asleep under the tree. She dreamt that two knights came to her and bade her come speak with their lord and king. When she refused to go with them, they returned bringing their king, a thousand knights, and many beautiful women dressed in white and riding snow-white horses. The king's clothing glittered; he wore a crown that sparkled in the sun. He guided a white horse with an empty saddle that seemed prepared for someone. In her dream, Heurodis knew that it was prepared for her, and she climbed onto the steed. Together, she and the Fairy King, for it was he who appeared in her dream, rode off with all the handsome knights and the lovely ladies to a beautiful country where there were flowers of every kind, lush meadows of grass and clover, forests, lakes, and clear blue sky. Above all of this, surrounded by wonderful rose gardens and apple orchards, was the palace of the Fairy King. He showed her all of this in her dreams and then returned her to where she slept under the imp tree. He told her to return to the tree the next day at the same time or she would die.

When Heurodis awoke, Orfeo was standing beside her, much concerned about how she had tossed and turned in her sleep. She told him of her dream, and he told her that when she returned the next day to the tree, he would surround her with a thousand knights, their swords drawn to protect her from being abducted by Fairy King. When the time came the next day, the knights were in place, swords drawn, surrounding Heurodis under the tree. But the Fairy King snatched her away nonetheless, undeterred by all the knights and swords. Heurodis went to live in the palace of the Fairy King.

Orfeo searched everywhere for his beloved Heurodis. He could find no sign of her anywhere because she was in the land of the fairies and not on earth. In utter despair, he left his palace and ceased to be king of his own land. He went deep into the forest, carrying only a harp to keep him company. For years, Orfeo remained deep in the forest, playing his harp and singing songs filled with sorrow for his lost love. The wild beasts were enchanted and came to hear him play. He was often surrounded by a fox, a bear, and even little squirrels, who were enraptured by his sorrowful music. At times Orfeo thought he saw the Fairy King, sometimes with his knights ready for war, sometimes preparing for the hunt, and sometimes dancing a joyful dance. But there was never any sign of Heurodis.

One day Orfeo's chance came. Sixty ladies came into the forest riding snow-white horses, and in the midst of them rode his beloved queen, Heurodis. Orfeo was determined to follow them at day's end. Carrying his harp, he followed them through a wild rocky place and between two cliffs on a path overhung with heavy branches. They rode their horses slowly, chatting and laughing, unaware of Orfeo with his harp following them on foot. After many miles, Orfeo came to the fairest country he had ever seen. He saw the lakes and forest, the gardens and meadows, and above it all, the palace. Even though it was nighttime, the precious stones in the palace walls gave off a brilliant light.

Wanting desperately to retrieve his lost love, Orfeo strode into the palace hall and found the King of Fairies on his throne. The King of Fairies was at first enraged to see Orfeo, but then he saw the harp. "Play something beautiful for us all!" the Fairy King demanded.

Orfeo began to play, pouring out songs of love for Heurodis and his hopes for her return. Heurodis herself was filled with longing at the sound of Orfeo's music. The Fairy King was so enchanted by the sound that he promised to Orfeo any gift he liked. Orfeo had one word in reply, "Heurodis!"

The King of Fairies gave Heurodis back to Orfeo and the two of them returned hand in hand with great joy back through the wilderness to their own kingdom, where they remained together in peace and happiness for the rest of their lives. And together they warned everyone in the kingdom to never sleep under the imp tree in the orchard again.

## Meaning and Wisdom for Unitarian Universalists

### Hearing a Calling

It takes time for Orfeo to find Heurodis and to win her back from the King of Fairies. Orfeo leaves his kingdom and retreats, spending years in the forest exploring the heights and depths of his love, and enchanting the animals in the forest with his songs. He prepares himself for the eventual bid for Heurodis's return by learning to play his harp. He learns to pour his love into song, taking a peaceful, creative approach to winning her back. This story calls us to take time to reflect and retreat when we face a big challenge. Sometimes we must gather and nurture our creative powers before we are ready to summon what is needed for the journey ahead.

### Opening to New Revelation

In this story, Orfeo's love for Heurodis ultimately holds the key to winning her back. He is unable to keep her with the help of a thousand knights with drawn swords; force of arms utterly fails him in keeping Heurodis close at hand. It is the love held in Orfeo's beautiful music that draws Heurodis away from the magical land of the fairies and so impresses the King of Fairies that he is willing to give her up. This story reveals to us the wisdom that one does not protect and nurture love by force of arms or by demanding compliance with one's own wishes, but rather by opening one's heart to another.

### Finding Wisdom Through the Principles and Sources

This is a story that ends with peace and happiness for all in both the Fairy Kingdom and in Orfeo's and Heurodis's world. It speaks to a vision of conflicts resolved without violence. It is about the power of love and of the creative process to bring about change, a world with peace, liberty, and justice for all.

## Connecting with Our Lives

### In Our Faith Communities

This story invites exploration. Create a fairy kingdom together; paint a large poster or build a model of the kingdom with its palace and its lovely grounds. As children create, engage them in conversation about how Orfeo finds a way to bring Heurodis back. The hero's journey takes him deep into himself to find another way to resolve a conflict that the sword fails to solve. Even with a thousand knights and a thousand drawn swords, he is unable to prevent the King of Fairies from abducting Heurodis. It is his love for Heurodis and the music he learns to create to express that love that ultimately make the difference. Invite children to share stories about times when they have used creative ways to solve a conflict.

Invite a harpist to share music with the children. Suggest that they imagine Orfeo learning to play his songs and the enchantment of the animals as they listen. Using animal puppets, re-create this part of the story, with the harpist playing the role of Orfeo. Engage the children in conversation about why music is so enchanting, and ask them to share stories from their own experience. If you have budding musicians in the group, invite them to share a piece of music with the others.

### At Home

Engage in family conversation about why the swords don't stop the King of Fairies from taking Heurodis. Why is music able to do something that swords cannot? Introduce the famous adage written in 1830 by Edward Bulwer-Lytton: "The pen is mightier than the sword." What does that mean? Consider with children the wisdom that this adage and the story offer about solving conflicts in a peaceful, creative way.

Explore making music or visual art together as a family, without pressure of time. Sing songs together or play rhythm or other instruments. Create a family collage or other work of art. Allow yourself to feel the peace and enchantment of the creative process.

# We Are All One

This story is based on a folktale from the Canton (Kwantung) Province of China and is often referred to as "The Miracle Bead." Re-created by Lawrence Yep, this version brings the sensibility of the American immigrant experience to the tale. Yep believes the tale resonates for Chinese American immigrants who, far away from their home villages, have worked hard at reestablishing connections in a new place and at being "one" with other Chinese immigrants. In this abridged version of Yep's telling, a kind peddler learns about his connection with all of life. He searches for a magic bead and receives help from a community of insects almost invisible to others in the hurry of their daily lives.

"We Are All One" echoes the immigrant experience of communities of wisdom that may be unnoticed to those outside them. Critic Celestine Woo states that Yep's tales "do not merely recall the old country, but transform and attain new meaning when transplanted to a bicultural environment." Like many good wisdom tales, "We Are All One" offers lessons for all of us, immigrants or not.

Once upon a time there was a very rich man who had a disease in his eyes. No matter how much he spent on medicines and doctors, nothing was found to cure his ailment. Desperate, he offered a large reward to anyone who could bring him a cure.

In the same city there lived a peddler who was kind but very poor. He had once heard of a miracle herb that might cure the rich man's disease. He decided to go into the woods to see if he could find it.

He left early one morning and began to search everywhere for the herb that might cure eyesight. He came upon a tiny stream on his travels. Looking closely, he observed that a rock had blocked the stream, damming it up and flooding a nearby ants' nest. He took a sharp stick and dug a new channel for the water, sending it away from the ants and their nest. "We are all one," he said aloud as he rescued the ants.

As the peddler searched, he found himself further and further from home, and very tired. "Maybe I'll just lay down here and have a little nap," he thought. And he did.

While he slept, the peddler had a most peculiar dream. He found himself in a strange city, nothing like any he had ever seen before. In his dream, he stood before the ant queen. "Don't be frightened," she said. "You are here so that we can honor you! You tamed the great flood, saving our home. In return, you need only ask, and my people will help you whenever you need them." And in her most queen-like voice she announced, "We are all one."

When the peddler awoke from his strange dream, he realized that much of the day had passed. He wanted to continue his search, but he was far from home in a strange region. He knew he must find shelter for the night. He walked for some time longer, searching as he went for the miracle herb. Finally, in a clearing, he came across an old green-roofed temple. Although it had been many years since the temple had been used and the building was in terrible disrepair, it offered some shelter for the night. As he came close to the temple door, he saw a centipede, brightly colored with yellow dots on its sides, crawling as quickly as possible toward the same door. A bird was swooping down, intent on eating the small centipede. Saying, "We are all one," the peddler shooed away the bird and placed his hand next to the centipede so it crawled onto his palm. He carried the centipede gently inside the temple and gave it leaves to eat and a safe spot for resting. It was not long before darkness arrived and he fell asleep.

The peddler was awakened from his sleep in the temple by the sound of footsteps, and the noise of opening and closing doors. Though he could see nothing in the darkness, he heard a voice: "There is a tree south of here with two trunks, a most unusual tree. At its foot, next to the root, there is an old magic bead. A centipede spat on it long ago. If this bead were dissolved in wine and given to the rich man to drink then his eyes would be cured." Too tired to wonder about the voice, the tired peddler returned to sleep.

When daylight first entered the old temple, the peddler looked around, trying to find the source of the voice he had heard in the night. "Was that you speaking?" he asked the centipede, who was still nearby, enjoying his leaves. Perhaps it was, or perhaps it was all a dream.

The peddler spent most of the following day searching for the unusual tree. He searched high and low, around and around, and did not find it. As the day neared its end, he came to one more tree and leaned against it. It took some time before he realized that he was leaning against a tree with two trunks. He looked at the root, hopeful, but not really expecting to find anything there. What hope he had was dashed as he realized that his tired eyes could never find anything as small as a little bead among the leaves at the foot of the tree. He felt around in vain for the tiny treasure.

Then he had an idea. "Ants," he called. "Ants! Please come and help me find the bead. We are all one!" Ants came scurrying from everywhere, moving in and around and under the pile of leaves at the foot of the tree. To the peddler's delight, he saw two ants crawl out from under the leaves, each one carrying one end of a small bead. The magic bead!

After thanking the ants again and again, the peddler returned to his home, carefully carrying the tiny bead. He took it to the rich man and instructed him to dissolve it and drink. The rich man did just that, and his eyes were healed.

He rewarded the poor peddler handsomely, so that he lived in comfort for the rest of his days.

☙

## Meaning and Wisdom for Unitarian Universalists

*Hearing a Calling*

This folktale is about connection and unexpected gifts. Our Unitarian Universalist seventh Principle speaks of the interconnected web of existence of which we are part. In this tale, the peddler's kindness in saving the smallest of creatures is returned to him in turn by those creatures. We are called to care for each other. The refrain line, "We are all one," echoes the idea, deeply rooted in our Universalist tradition, that all creatures with whom we share this planet are reflections of the Divine, carriers of the Spirit of Life. We find meaning together.

*Opening to New Revelation*

In this tale, help for the peddler comes from totally unexpected sources. Attuned to that which surrounds him, he is able to "hear" and receive the help that is offered to him; he is open to revelation. Even though the help is magical, it is available to him only because he is paying attention and willing to trust gifts of wisdom and knowledge when they are presented to him.

*Finding Wisdom Through the Principles and Sources*

Meaning for us as Unitarian Universalists comes from the evolution of the tale itself. How does the wisdom of one culture find life in another? What is retained and what is reborn with new sensibility? How do we approach wisdom from a culture different from our own in a way that is respectful of its origins and its context? Our empathic connection with the peddler in this tale provides some clues. Needing others is a basic shared human experience, but how often do we hide this need? Often those who support us most are invisible to others. Yep locates this tale within the immigrant experience, but all listeners can relate to holding in their hearts communities and individuals that are worlds apart.

## Connecting with Our Lives

*In Our Faith Communities*

Literal aspects of this story may appeal to children. They may be inspired to look for hidden insect worlds, like the one that is so helpful to the peddler. Take a walk to look for insect life with children, and engage them in learning more about the worms, bugs, and other insects they see. How are people connected to insects? How do they enrich our lives? Invite children to create pictures of underground insect worlds.

Older children may enjoy reflecting on the story's idea of getting help from unexpected sources. Have they ever received good advice from someone or something that surprised them? Have children work together to help each person remember an instance of receiving unexpected help. Invite children to tell about a time when they received unexpected help, and record or videotape their stories to share with others as a reminder that we don't have to solve all of our problems all by ourselves.

*At Home*

Being open to learning from unexpected sources can be a spiritual act. Perhaps children have experienced knowing something intuitively; their inner voices can be a sort of spiritual compass. Help children honor the many sources of knowledge that are available to them.

The peddler receives advice while dreaming. In your family, invite children to share some of their own dreams. Have they ever solved a problem or found other wisdom while dreaming? Some individuals keep a journal to record their dreams. Consider creating a family dream journal, where the most interesting and fantastic of dreams are recorded.

# Our Unitarian Universalist Sources

*The living tradition we share draws from many sources:*

Direct experience of that transcending mystery and wonder, affirmed in all cultures, which moves us to a renewal of the spirit and an openness to the forces that create and uphold life;

Words and deeds of prophetic women and men which challenge us to confront powers and structures of evil with justice, compassion and the transforming power of love;

Wisdom from the world's religions which inspires us in our ethical and spiritual life;

Jewish and Christian teachings which call us to respond to God's love by loving our neighbors as ourselves;

Humanist teachings which counsel us to heed the guidance of reason and the results of science, and warn us against idolatries of the mind and spirit;

Spiritual teachings of Earth-centered traditions which celebrate the sacred circle of life and instruct us to live in harmony with the rhythms of nature.

# The Christmas Truce

This is a true story about a spontaneous Christmas ceasefire along the five-hundred-mile western front of World War I. Young men had been recruited across Europe to fight in the Great War, sold on the glorious adventure that awaited them. At the western front, they learned about the realities of warfare and left the illusions of glory behind. For a brief moment in this 1914 story, enemy soldiers on both sides recognized one another's humanity and shared a Christmas celebration.

Because the spontaneous truce happened all along the battle line, there are many eyewitness accounts; they differ in details but not in spirit. What is clear is that something wondrous overtook the young men at the front that Christmas Eve and allowed them to put aside their warring to make room for one another. Was it that the gifts from home had made the men nostalgic for a time before the war? Was it the Christmas music shared between the two factions? Was it the bravery of those who first stepped into No Man's Land that inspired the others to follow? Whatever created that moment, it left its mark on every person present. This story of the triumph of the Christmas spirit over the dehumanizing conditions of warfare affirms the presence of hope, joy, and love even under the most trying of circumstances.

When the Great War, which we now call World War I, started in Europe, many young men were eager to fight. Just out of school, they joined up with their schoolmates to go off on an exciting adventure. War seemed glorious in the fall of 1914 when young men from the British Empire went to France to fight against young men from the German Empire.

It did not take long for the new soldiers to discover the realities of war. Both sides dug trenches in the ground a few hundred feet from each other in France and in Belgium. Between the trenches was a flat open space called No Man's Land. Young men hid in the trenches day after day as gunfire came from snipers or artillery on one side or the other. To lift your head up out of a trench was to risk getting shot. Worst of all were the days when it rained. Soldiers were trapped in muddy, wet trenches, with the task of endless digging, as they tried to keep ahead of the floodwaters. When winter approached, there was more and more rain, and the trenches of both the German army and the British army were wet, cold, miserable mud holes.

As the soldiers huddled in their miserable trenches, they began to wonder about the enemy soldiers so close by. Bored soldiers shouted at each other back and forth between the trenches, calling names and taunting one another. Each side sang patriotic songs and folk songs to remind them of home. The two armies were close enough to hear one another's music. Always, there were the rifles and the machine guns, firing at any sign of movement outside the trench.

Back home, people in Germany and Britain thought often of their soldiers. They wanted to be sure that the soldiers had Christmas gifts, candies, cigarettes, letters, and photographs from home. German families sent their soldiers packages of gifts, letters, and photos. They also sent Christmas trees to the soldiers, who put them on top of the sandbags protecting the fronts of the trenches. The British saw all the Christmas trees and wondered if some kind of surprise attack were being planned. They watched and waited. The British people also sent letters, candies, and gifts to their soldiers. Each one received a small brass box embossed with a profile of Princess Mary of England. The box was full of cigarettes and had a card inside saying: "With best wishes for a happy Christmas and a victorious New Year from the Princess Mary and friends at home."

Christmas Eve arrived in 1914 and soldiers on both sides opened their packages in the muddy trenches and wished with all their hearts to be home again. They began singing carols and making merry—as merry as one can be in a trench—when something extraordinary happened.

Someone began to sing "Silent Night" in German, or perhaps "O Come All Ye Faithful" in English. In any event, the soldiers on the other side joined in the singing. The songs of the two armies, sung in two different languages, blended together in the starry night. Soon, a German soldier emerged from his trench. Everyone held his breath, but no one fired. He had a sign that said, "Merry Christmas! We not shoot. You not shoot." It wasn't long before a British soldier made his way into No Man's Land, then another, and another. Soon all the soldiers had climbed out of the trenches and were greeting one another, enemy greeting enemy, in the middle of No Man's Land. Officers tried in vain to forbid this from happening. Embodying the Christmas spirit of peace and good will, the men traded candies, swapped buttons from their uniforms, and showed one another pictures of families back home. Someone even started a soccer game, using an old ball and helmets to mark the goal posts.

The unplanned Christmas truce happened all along the five-hundred-mile battlefront. Whether it lasted a few hours or a few days, it gave each man pause as he learned that the enemy was a human being like himself. It was a time when the spirit of love and joy reigned supreme even in the midst of the battlefield.

## Meaning and Wisdom for Unitarian Universalists

### Hearing a Calling

In this story, young men at war experience something that changes the way they think about the enemy. What makes them engage with each other? This story calls us to recognize the humanity of all people, whether friend or foe, ally or enemy. We yearn for connection. Attending to another's point of view is a spiritual practice. Casting aside circumstances of politics and protocol, the soldiers are able to be faithful to what is most deeply in their hearts.

### Opening to New Revelation

Young men who went off expecting glorious adventure come face to face with the realities of muddy trenches and sniper fire, but they do not lose their humanity. Day in and day out as they face the trials of a bloody war, they do what they need to do to keep their spirits alive: celebrating, sharing stories, and singing. It is the language of music that touches their souls that Christmas Eve and allows them to figuratively and literally cross the divide that separates them. Music, stories, and moments of celebration can also open our souls to one another and to the joy of being alive.

### Finding Wisdom Through the Principles and Sources

Each of us has experienced moments when we have become part of something bigger and more important than ourselves. These are times when the spirit that moves us collectively transcends us as individuals. Transformation comes for us when we are part of a group that acts together out of love or courage or joy. Our faith tradition names that feeling of transcendence, mystery, and wonder as an important source of wisdom.

## Connecting with Our Lives

*In Our Faith Communities*
This story is loved by people of all ages. Share it with the wider congregation. It can be dramatized by older children as a Christmas play or retold as part of a worship service in the children's own words. Children may enjoy the chance to learn familiar carols in another language. You can listen to a piece of music about these events by John McCutcheon, entitled "Christmas in the Trenches."

Invite children to talk about the story's events. Why do they happen? What allows the soldiers to stop thinking of one another as enemies, even for a moment? What can we learn from this story about how to stop feuds between people or feuds between nations?

This story invites us to remember that there are those in our world caught up in war and violence. If there are people in your congregation or from your local area serving in war, children and families can send them holiday greetings. You might also highlight for children how participation in the Unitarian Universalist Service Committee's programs, including Guest at Your Table, helps people who are hurt by war and violence.

*At Home*
Children may need time to dwell on this story and they may ask whether it is true. Answer their questions about the story, helping them to visualize what happened. Invite speculation about why the soldiers take the risk of moving into No Man's Land. Many eyewitnesses said that it was the Christmas spirit that overtook everyone that night. What is the Christmas spirit? When have you felt that spirit? Share with one another stories from your own lives.

Choose one or more ways your family can remember and help those who are caught up in violence and war. Support an organization that helps refugees and others in war zones. Send letters and greetings to soldiers from your local area who have had to go to war. Remember in your family chalice lighting or grace at mealtime those whose lives are damaged by war and violence.

# For the Love of Stars

It is not often that we have the great joy of discovering one of our Unitarian Universalist forebears, but such is the case with Cecilia Payne-Gaposchkin. She was a twentieth-century astronomer whose important work sadly remains largely unattributed to her. A woman in a male-dominated field, she made significant contributions to astronomy while being paid a pittance as observatory staff and editor of observatory publications. Others were credited for her work. Passed over time and again due to her gender for promotions and for a well-deserved professorship, she continued to take joy in her research and in collaboration with many of the great scientific minds of her time.

Cecilia Payne-Gaposchkin's writings reveal a person who was truly in love with the universe and with the wonder of observation and discovery. Direct experience of transcending mystery and wonder was a way of life for her. In her writing she called her laboratory her chapel. She called her scientific work of observing, classifying, and puzzling out patterns, a kind of worship.

Cecilia was a wife and a mother of three children. She enrolled her children in the Sunday School at First Parish Unitarian Universalist in Lexington, Massachusetts, and like most parents took her turn as a Sunday School teacher. Her daughter Katherine recalls a Sunday when it was so cold that the car would not start. Cecilia bundled up warmly and walked three and a half miles to the church to teach her class.

Our Unitarian Universalist tradition finds no conflict between science and religion, and welcomes discoveries about the natural world in the search for truth and meaning. In her autobiography, Cecilia Payne-Gaposchkin describes her early years filled by her love of the stars and the natural world. The wisdom story that follows is largely drawn from these descriptions. It is a story of a brilliant and profoundly spiritual scientist who sets her sights on the universe itself. It is a story of a woman who follows her calling almost single-mindedly, undeterred by the barriers set forth due to her gender. It is in many ways a love story that speaks to the naturalist and the scientist in all of us.

Once there was a little girl named Cecilia who fell in love with the universe. She felt her heart leap with joy every time she learned something new about the world around her. She would grow up to become a scientist, an astronomer who studied the stars. Throughout her whole life, she studied and observed the stars, working with other scientists and on her own. What are stars made of? How are they born? Do they die? And how do we know? Throughout her whole life, her heart sang with each discovery, each bit of new understanding about the wonders of the far-off sky.

When Cecilia was a small child in England, still being pushed in a pram, which is an old-fashioned stroller, she saw a meteorite blaze across the sky. Her mother taught her a small rhyme so she could remember what it was:

"As we were walking home that night
We saw a shining meteorite."

She later told a friend that from that moment, she knew she would grow up to be an astronomer. She learned the names of all the constellations in the sky, picking out the Big Dipper, Orion's Belt, and others. She was naturally very observant and precise, able to pick out and remember small details. By age twelve, she had learned to measure things and to do math problems very precisely. At her school, they had an interesting way of increasing the students' powers of observation. Once a week, students were required to find with their eyes (not touching) three little brass tacks scattered somewhere in the school garden. For Cecilia, always an observer, this education just strengthened her resolve to be a scientist.

In 1912, when Cecilia was a teenager, there was very little help available for a young woman who wanted to be a scientist. Filled with joy and wonder, she studied the chemical elements that made up the world and learned to classify and identify plants of all kinds. She spent hours in a laboratory, which she called her chapel, where she conducted "a little worship service of her own," in awe before the magnificence of the natural world. Persistent, she found people who would teach her science at school, and she pored over her family's home library until she found two lonely science books to study: one about plants and the other containing Sir Isaac Newton's observations about planets and his law of gravity.

In 1919 Cecilia entered college to study botany, because the study of plants was an acceptable scientific study for a woman in those days. She went through her courses in botany, but also attended lectures in physics, where she found "pure delight." She was transformed by each new bit of knowledge about physics and astronomy. When she realized at one lecture that all motion is relative, she did not sleep for three nights. Leaving botany behind, she persuaded the college to allow her to take a degree in physics, because the astronomy she loved was considered part of physics.

After finishing her degree, Cecilia Payne left for the United States, where she would study as an astronomer at Harvard University. She spent her first two years there figuring out what stars are made of, and concluded in 1925 that most stars are primarily hydrogen. In today's world of satellites and computers, we know this to be true, but it was an extraordinary statement at that time. No one believed her. Nonetheless, when she presented those conclusions, she was the first person ever, male or female, to be awarded a Ph.D. in astronomy.

Cecilia had no small number of struggles as an astronomer because she was a woman. It took until 1956—after twenty-three years of working—for her to be named a professor. Even so, she was the first woman ever to be named a full professor at Harvard. When she was thirty-four, she arranged for the rescue of Russian astronomer Sergei Gaposchkin, who had been exiled from his own country. She later married him and they did research together. They raised three children, who all went to Sunday School at First Parish Unitarian Universalist in Lexington, Massachusetts. Through it all, she held on to her love for the scientific quest—and for the stars.

Near the end of her life, Cecilia wrote that where other women were not allowed to be "in direct touch with the fountain-head, whether you call it God or the Universe," she had been—always. Her love for the universe and for the wonder of it all lasted her entire life.

## Meaning and Wisdom for Unitarian Universalists

### Hearing a Calling

Cecilia Payne-Gaposchkin's story is all about her calling. She is drawn to the natural world, a world that becomes larger and larger as she explores it more. She is hungry for new knowledge, asking questions, seeking out resources, observing and puzzling out the world. She enthusiastically takes her place among the scientific community of the time, building on the work of others and seeking to add her own insights. This is her spiritual quest. New discoveries feed her soul. Her story calls us to pay attention to our passions. It also calls us to the practice of taking the time to observe and let our hearts leap with joy at the beauty and intricacy of our world and the universe.

### Opening to New Revelation

Cecilia's way of living is to actively seek knowledge. Each new thing she learns, whether by reading, listening, or research, opens the way for deeper understanding. She writes in her autobiography: "It is well for us that knowledge comes to us gradually. If we were faced with the full complexity of the facts at the beginning of our search, we should be so bewildered that we might well give up in despair." Her work reminds us that understanding comes slowly. We build on those who came before us and bequeath to those who will come after.

Cecilia Payne-Gaposchkin discovered that stars were mostly made of hydrogen, but many senior astronomers discouraged her from putting forth that conclusion. As a result, she downplayed her findings in her dissertation. Allowing herself to be dissuaded set her back some years in her research, and she later expressed regret for not standing more firmly by her observations, data, and calculations. She urged scientists training with her not to back down simply because someone authoritative questioned their ideas.

### Finding Wisdom Through the Principles and Sources

Cecilia Payne-Gaposchkin's story invites us to see scientific research as a route to "direct experience of transcending mystery and wonder." She unabashedly writes of her work in spiritual terms and sees the long hours of compiling and puzzling out data as hours at worship. To Cecilia, science is not just about conclusions and new, dramatic theories but about immersing one's self in exploration for the love of the quest. This path fully embraces the spiritual experience of the scientist.

## Connecting with Our Lives

### In Our Faith Communities

The story of Cecilia Payne-Gaposchkin is remarkable but largely unknown. Engage children in educating the congregation about this Unitarian Universalist forebear via posters, displays, a newsletter article, or other means. Children will enjoy taking the lead and the congregation will benefit as well.

The details of Payne-Gaposchkin's work are complex. Invite a physicist or astronomer to tell about the kind of work they do, or visit a local observatory for a tour with a child-friendly guide. Help children understand that much of what Cecilia did was done with very simple equipment, before computers and satellites. Ask your tour guide or visitor to explain how the study of stars is different now than it was twenty-five or so years ago, when she was at the end of her career, or ninety years ago, when she was beginning. This story lends itself to Internet exploration of photos from the Hubble telescope and child-friendly websites about the stars and the planets.

*At Home*

Explore the world of astronomy with your family. A trip to an observatory or laboratory, online resources, or stargazing with an amateur astronomer will enrich this story. Simply taking time to look with wonder and attention at the night sky may be the most powerful follow-up activity of all. One of the important parts of Cecilia Payne-Gaposchkin's story is her attitude of wonder and awe, and her love for knowledge. Honor the naturalist and the scientist in each of us. Help children develop questions, wonderings, observations, and exploration when out in the natural world.

Families can also talk about Cecilia's story as a tale of overcoming obstacles, many of them due to her gender. What might she have accomplished if it had not been so difficult for her to be seen as a brilliant leader in the field of astronomy? Are there times today when people are prevented by prejudice or other obstacles from making a fuller contribution to the world?

# Rosa Parks

We all think we know the story of Rosa Parks. The standard script tells of a woman who became tired of discrimination and injustice and one day just refused to budge from her bus seat, an individual with courage who sparked the civil rights movement. But December 1, 1955, was not an isolated moment in the life of Rosa Parks. The complete story of how she reached that day is far more interesting than the simple version. Her life and experiences made that moment possible, but so did the passion of the many others who worked to overturn injustice and discrimination.

This story presents Rosa Parks as a young woman with great integrity and humility. She is willing to take her place among those working for justice, doing whatever it takes to advance the cause, including answering phones and stuffing envelopes. She takes time to learn from others who have come before, to be grounded in the history and culture of a grassroots movement. She serves as a mentor to teens, organizing youth conferences and other events. She is a collaborator, participating in trainings and strategy sessions designed to determine the most effective way to move forward. The full picture of Rosa Parks is quite different from the snapshot many hold, in which she simply refuses to move from her seat on the bus on December 1, 1955.

This is a story of hope. It invites each of us to make our own contributions, large and small, to making the world a better place. Read or tell it as though sharing a compelling story from the life of a beloved and familiar person, because that is exactly what you are doing.

On December 1, 1955, in Montgomery, Alabama, an African American woman named Rosa Parks refused to give up her seat on the bus to a white man. She was arrested on the spot and her arrest sparked the beginning of the U.S. civil rights movement. That is the way many of us have heard the story. But she did not act alone. She had spent a lifetime acquiring the skills, wisdom, and experience she needed at that very moment. She was one person in a grand organization of people working for equality and justice. She was the right person at the right time, but she was not alone.

The daughter of Louise, a teacher, and James, a carpenter, Rosa Parks was born in Tuskegee, Alabama, in 1913, a time when black people were subject to unfair laws and unequal treatment at every turn. Her mother believed strongly that one should take advantage of every opportunity, so she enrolled Rosa in Miss White's School for Girls. There she was taught that she could do anything she wanted to do, even though that seemed impossible for an African American child in the southern United States at that time. When Miss White's School closed, Rosa was fifteen. She took in sewing and cleaned houses to help support her family, and tried to complete her high school education. Family illnesses made it impossible for her to finish on time, although she did earn her diploma three years later.

When Rosa was eighteen, she met Raymond Parks and married him a year later. He was a barber who was active in politics and in the cause of justice and equality for African American people. From him, she learned that there were people working hard to get rid of unfair laws. With him, she joined and became active in the NAACP, the National Association for the Advancement of Colored People. She served as the volunteer secretary for the NAACP Montgomery branch, coming in after work to answer phones, address envelopes, take meeting notes, or do whatever needed doing. She met other activists who mentored her and taught her about the long, proud history of the civil rights movement. In time, she became the youth leader of the branch, working with teens and passing on her own knowledge and wisdom.

Those were extraordinary times. In 1954, the U. S. Supreme Court had declared that the laws requiring separate schools for black and white children were unjust and unconstitutional. The NAACP leadership knew that something dramatic would happen— and soon. African Americans would not wait forever for just treatment. In March of 1955, an African American teenager named Claudette Colvin, a teenager from Rose Parks's NAACP youth group, refused to give up her seat on the bus to a white man and was arrested. The NAACP leaders thought that maybe the time had come for action to force just treatment, but they knew that Claudette was only fifteen years old and had been in some trouble, so they decided not to press the issue. They needed just the right person to refuse to yield her seat, a pillar of the community, one who could withstand intense pressure and not lose her cool.

In the summer of 1955, the NAACP sent Rosa Parks and others to the Highlander Folk School for a ten-day training session in nonviolent protest. There she learned of Mahatma Gandhi's commitment to and use of nonviolence in India. She learned more of the history of the civil rights movement. She met the movers and shakers of the movement and sang its powerful songs, including "We Shall Overcome" and "Keep Your Eyes on the Prize." After twelve years of working hard as an NAACP volunteer and leader, she had now acquired the skills and background she would need when the moment came.

And come it did. On December 1, 1955, Rosa Parks, seated in the front row of the "colored" section of a bus, refused to give up that seat when the bus became crowded and there wasn't enough room for all the white people to sit. She refused to move and she was arrested. The NAACP leadership and Rosa herself understood that the time for action had arrived. She was a pillar of the community, a person of wisdom, skill, maturity, and character who could weather what lay ahead. Four days later, the Montgomery bus boycott began and the civil rights movement came to the attention of people across the United States.

Rosa Parks died in 2005 after a long and full life. She is a hero in the United States, remembered for her courage, dignity, and determination. The memory of her life and deeds speak to us of her wisdom, strategic skill, passion, and membership in a great community of activist souls.

## Meaning and Wisdom for Unitarian Universalists

### Hearing a Calling

Rosa Parks's life embodies a sense of calling. Her call to make a difference in the world resulted in a lifelong commitment that took many forms. She was a follower, collaborator, mentor, strategist, and leader, willing to bring all of her passion and skills to bear in the work of strengthening justice. We are called to do no less in our own lives.

### Opening to New Revelation

Often the heroes in our culture seem to possess courage, strength, and wisdom in far greater measure than ordinary people. Believing that those who do extraordinary things are somehow larger than life and that they act alone leaves us with the sense that we ourselves do not have what it takes to make a difference in the world. The story of Rosa Parks reveals something different. Each of us has a contribution to make to justice, and we don't have to do it alone. We do not have to begin by having all the answers or knowing exactly how to proceed. Justice requires the efforts of many over the long haul. We are each needed and necessary.

### Finding Wisdom Through the Principles and Sources

Rosa Parks was a prophet in our time, one whose style was not to be an orator denouncing injustice, but rather to work quietly, mostly behind the scenes, preparing for the moment when what was required was that she hold her ground. Her style of prophethood reminds us that learning about issues, acquiring important skills, practicing collaboration, and growing our own souls is vital work that allows us to take our place in the long line of people working for justice.

## Connecting with Our Lives

### In Our Faith Communities

Engage children in conversation about Rosa Parks. What have they learned from study at school? How is what they have learned different from this telling of the story? Does it change the story of the civil rights movement to know that people had been working and strategizing for a long time before the Montgomery bus boycott? Explore the story of E.D. Nixon, Rosa Parks's mentor, who was head of both the Montgomery branch of the NAACP and the Brotherhood of Sleeping Car Porters in 1955 . Youth can view the film "10,000 Black Men Named George" about A. Philip Randolph and the organizing of the Pullman porters in the 1920s, as a way of helping them to understand some earlier civil rights efforts.

Whom do children think of as heroes? What kinds of qualities do their heroes have? How do they make the world a better place? Can athletes be heroes? How was Rosa Parks a hero? Invite children to name all of the qualities they think heroes display and to create a collage with words and pictures that point to those qualities. Engage children in conversation about ways in which they, too, display heroic qualities.

### At Home

Engage in conversation with your family about the real story behind Rosa Parks's famous moment on the bus. Did you ever wonder if people before Rosa Parks and Dr. Martin Luther King resisted injustice? How does knowing this story change the way you picture the events? How did people prepare themselves for the challenges of leadership and service in the civil rights movement?

What preparations are you making in your life today for a time when you are called to take a stand?

Find out about your local NAACP branch and what they are doing to resist injustice. Volunteer to help with a voter registration drive or other project of that group. Teenagers and adults in the family can learn a great deal about current issues concerning African Americans and about some current antidiscrimination efforts from the NAACP magazine *Crisis*, which can be found online at www.thecrisismagazine.com.

What does your family do to work for justice? Through your congregation or another organization, get your family involved in working for justice for all people.

# Arius the Heretic

Many Unitarian Universalists rather enjoy being thought of as heretics, or holders of religious ideas contrary to the mainstream. Unitarian Universalists are the inheritors and guardians of a long tradition that has embraced heretics, a tradition that dates back to a Libyan priest named Arius who lived in the fourth century.

Arius lived during the time when the leaders of the Christian church, freed from persecution by the Edict of Milan in 312, were engaging in debates about the nature of humanity and the nature of Jesus. The Roman Empire was in crisis, pressured on many fronts by those who threatened to overrun it. There was a strong need to unify the Christian Church under the sovereignty of a protective savior. The Emperor Constantine viewed uniting the Christian Church as a way to strengthen and unify the Roman Empire and to bring order to the outlying areas. The endless religious debates, often leading to violence between partisans and riots in the street, were a source of significant annoyance to Constantine. In 325, he convened a council at his summer residence at Nicea, in what is now Turkey, insisting that the bishops agree on a creed that would bring unity to the church. By the close of the Council at Nicea, the Roman state and the Christian Church had reached a mutual understanding, with the emperor playing a significant role in the church and the church a significant role in the empire.

The priest Arius believed that Jesus was divine but somewhat less so than God. He believed that Jesus' wisdom and teachings were more important than his death and resurrection. Arius believed that human beings could draw closer to God by following those teachings. As the Christian Church solidified and unified in the fourth century and adopted a Trinitarian theology, Arianism became the archetypal heresy for the orthodox. Our Unitarian forebears in both Europe and North America were often accused of espousing Arianism.

This story reminds us that our tradition has a taproot that goes all the way back to the early Christian Church. It is a story that invites us to celebrate that heritage and to embrace the label *heretic*, which comes from a Greek word meaning "to choose." It is a remarkable and precious legacy.

There came a time when the Emperor Constantine had had it with all the arguing. As head of the vast Roman Empire, he called a halt to the persecutions and killings of those people known as Christians. The Christians were followers of Jesus of Nazareth, a Jewish prophet who had been put to death almost three hundred years earlier. They were known for taking care of one another, and of the poor, the sick, widows, and children in need of help. Constantine was interested in these Christians and their new religion—if only they would stop arguing!

The real trouble was in a place called Alexandria, in Egypt. There was a priest named Arius who was in charge of part of the Christian Church in Alexandria. He was tremendously popular, in part because he was also a poet and a singer. He sometimes taught or preached by putting lessons into poems and songs, which was much more fun and interesting for the people than just plain words. He was a favorite of sailors, dockworkers, and young people. Many flocked to hear him speak. They were convinced that following Jesus would help them to get closer to God. After all, Arius told them that Jesus had started out as a human being who was so holy that God had adopted him as a son.

Alexander, the main bishop of the city, was Arius's superior. He had a different idea about Jesus. He said that Jesus had been one with God since the very beginning, and that when he was on earth, he was God living as a human being. This bishop taught that people were basically sinful and that Jesus had come to earth and lived and died in order to save people from their wrongdoing. He also said that Arius was a heretic, which meant that Arius was preaching things that were different from what most bishops and church leaders believed to be true.

So arguments began and continued. Every day people debated at the market and in the public square. Sometimes there were even fistfights and riots about which view was the right one, Alexander's or Arius's. Word of all of this reached the Emperor Constantine, and he wanted the fighting stopped. It wasn't good for the empire if people were rioting in the streets, so Constantine decided to settle it once and for all. He called a council and invited all of the bishops in the empire to spend some months at his summer residence in Nicea, right beside a beautiful lake in what is now the country of Turkey.

And so the bishops arrived in May at this wonderful summer residence. Many traveled for a long time to get there, coming by ship and then overland to Nicea. Everything was ready for their arrival. Servants made sure that the food and drink were perfect and that the guests were truly pampered. The emperor looked resplendent in purple robes with gold adornment. He told the bishops to make up their minds about this question of Jesus. After this council, there was to be no more arguing! He wanted a strong

Roman empire with one religion. Constantine meant to enforce whatever the decision was with the power of his empire.

Alexander and his supporters spoke. They presented parts of the songs and poetry Arius had written, to prove he was a dangerous heretic, maybe even an agent of the devil. By the time they had finished, all but two of the hundred bishops were on Alexander's side, condemning Arius. Arius himself was not allowed to speak because he was only a priest, not a bishop. While they spent a few weeks enjoying the delights of the lakeside summer home, the bishops wrote a creed for the Christian Church, a set of beliefs that everyone needed to agree to in order to belong. All were required to sign it. Arius and the two bishops who supported him refused to sign it. They were declared heretics and sent into exile.

There were a few more councils and lots more violence over the next few years. Arius was in and out of trouble during that whole period of time, but he never gave up on what he thought was right and true. On the day he died, quite suddenly, he was with friends and foes, still holding fast to what he believed.

We remember Arius seventeen hundred years later. He is Arius the heretic, Arius the Christian, Arius the believer that humans could grow in wisdom and in spirit, and Arius who began our Unitarian history and tradition.

## Meaning and Wisdom for Unitarian Universalists

### Hearing a Calling

To be part of the Unitarian Universalist faith is to be part of a movement that has a deep and rich tradition going back to the early days of Christianity, when the nature of Jesus of Nazareth and the meaning of his life were hotly debated throughout the Roman Empire. This story calls us to embrace that heritage and honor the Arian heresy, which has survived the centuries, inspiring preachers and martyrs, public leaders and private people in generation

after generation who look to the religion of Jesus rather than the
religion about Jesus for wisdom and inspiration.

### Opening to New Revelation

While we may have difficulty understanding all the intricacies of
the theological debate that took place in the fourth-century Roman
Empire, two pictures of human nature emerge. Arius believed human beings to be basically good creatures who could follow the
wisdom and teachings of Jesus and aspire to the same perfection.
The mainstream position was that human beings were sinful creatures in need of salvation. Proponents of this theological point
of view held that the main story about Jesus was the story of his
passion, crucifixion, and resurrection to save humanity from sin.
The same debate about the nature of people—basically good or
basically sinful—has engaged civilizations for thousands of years.
It is still relevant in our personal lives and in the public square.
What do you think about this basic question? If you believe people
to be basically good, how do you account for some of the unspeak-
able evils of human history?

### Finding Wisdom Through the Principles and Sources

Arius's refusal to sign the Nicene Creed reminds us that our creed-
less faith echoes back to early Christian times. There are no creedal
tests for Unitarian Universalist faith; we honor individual decisions
and conscience. It is this longstanding practice that gave rise to our
modern day theological diversity and our promise, encapsulated
in the third Principle, to accept one another and encourage each
other to grow spiritually.

## Connecting with Our Lives

### In Our Faith Communities

In this story, the emperor and the church leaders decide that it is
important for everyone who is part of a church to agree to believe
the same things. This is not true in Unitarian Universalist congre-

gations. Invite children and adults to make a list on newsprint of all the things about their faith community that people in the group agree on, and another list of things where there is disagreement. What kinds of agreements are necessary for our faith community to be healthy? About what kinds of things can we disagree?

Tell the story of Arius and the Council of Nicea by acting out the great debate in the Council. The major characters in the play are the Emperor Constantine, Bishop Alexander and those who agree with him, and those who agree with Arius. Engage the group in deciding what the arguments will be in advance of the reenactment. At the time of the reenactment, invite the audience to respond as though at a sporting event to arguments on both sides, with some supporting those who state that "Jesus is God" and some supporting those who state "Jesus was a holy man." Those two statements are simplifications of the theological arguments, but they are statements children can understand.

### At Home

Explore the term *heretic* and what it means to be part of a tradition that has embraced heretics across the centuries. Unitarian Universalist children may have trouble understanding that in some faith communities, one has to believe a specific set of statements about the nature of God in order to belong. Engage your family in conversation about what holds Unitarian Universalists together. What do we agree on? Guide the conversation toward the conclusion that our agreement to *act* in certain ways holds us together, not our agreement to *believe* in certain ways.

# The Mustard Seed Medicine

Unitarian Universalist faith holds us in the cycle of life. Growing, becoming, and dying are all part of the human experience. A primary function of our faith communities is responding to these experiences, including death. How do we care for those who are dying? How do we acknowledge the end of a life? How do we care for those who grieve? How do we honor and celebrate the legacy of one who is now gone and offer what is needed for the mourners and the community to move forward after a loss?

We are not eager to broach the topic of death with children. The discovery of a dead bird or mouse in the backyard or neighborhood can launch conversation. We might be forced into talk when a beloved pet is ill and must be euthanized. The conversation might begin with a decision about whether to bring a child to the wake or funeral of an elderly relative. However it happens, there comes a time when all of us must confront the reality of death.

It is a gift to children to provide an opportunity to talk about death at a time when they are not grieving. "The Mustard Seed Medicine," a well-known story from the Buddhist tradition, is a comforting tale that acknowledges that death is not an aberration but part of our families and communities. It teaches us a way to respond with compassion to our own grief and to the sorrow of others.

Once upon a time there lived a young mother whose name was Kisa Gotami. She had a son whom she loved above all else in the world. She loved him when he was happy and cooperative and she loved him when he was grumpy and whiney. She even loved him when he had tantrums.

There came a time when the young boy became very ill. Doctors and healers were not able to cure him, and he died. Kisa was beside herself with grief. She picked up the boy's body and wrapped it in blankets, carrying it about the village asking everyone she met if they knew how to bring her son back to life. One kind friend suggested that she visit the Buddha, the Enlightened One, who would surely be able to help her.

Kisa approached the Buddha, carrying her son's body and weeping. "Please help me! Please tell me how to bring my son back to life."

The Buddha looked at her and felt great compassion. "I can help you," he said. "But first you must bring me some mustard seed from a home where no loved one has ever died, no parent or grandparent, no brother or sister, no child or much-loved friend." Sensing hope for the first time since her son had died, Kisa went back home and laid her son's body on the bed. She set out to find some mustard seed.

The first place Kisa visited was the house next door. She knocked on the door and waited. When her neighbor came to the door, Kisa asked for a handful of mustard seed.

"Why, of course, Kisa. I'll be right back."

As the neighbor woman was about to hand her the mustard seed, Kisa remembered to ask if anyone from the household had ever died.

"Kisa, don't you remember? My father died a year ago, and we were sad for a long time. We still miss him."

Dejected, Kisa went away without taking the mustard seed.

When Kisa visited a second house and asked for mustard seed, that neighbor reminded her that a beloved niece had died in that house five years ago. Sadly, Kisa went away without any mustard seed.

So Kisa proceeded from house to house, visiting every home in the village. At each stop, the family spoke of a nephew, a mother, a grandparent, or a beloved child who had died. Each family told a tale of grief and loss.

When she had visited the last house in the village, it became clear to Kisa that what the Buddha had asked her to do was impossible. She was overcome with sadness and could not go any further. She found a banyan tree at the edge of the village and sat down to cry.

Kisa cried for hours. Over time, though, a strange peace came over her. She thought about all the stories she had heard that day, of loved ones who had died and of families who had experienced terrible sadness. She realized that she was not alone in experiencing the death of someone she loved. She was not alone in her grief and her sadness.

The next day she returned to the Buddha. When she told him of her search for the mustard seed that could not be found, he nodded. "Our lives in this world are not permanent. Each one of us must die, some at a young age and some older. All of us will know times of great happiness and times of deep sorrow. Do not try to keep free yourself from these human experiences. Try instead to be kind and compassionate to all beings, enjoying all the gifts that life brings."

As time passed, Kisa became a comforter of all who experienced sadness and death. Even though she always missed her son, she learned to accept his death and to take comfort in knowing that she was not alone in her grief.

## Meaning and Wisdom for Unitarian Universalists

### Hearing a Calling

Kisa Gotami's neighbors do not know how to respond to her. Because of their own experiences with death, they are unable to provide the mustard seed she needs. Because of her own intense grief, she is unable to remember that others in her village have also suffered loss. Her neighbors are not offended; they deeply understand Kisa's grief.

This story reminds us of something we already know, that death and grief come to all of us in turn. It calls us to take the time to respond to one another in times of mourning, to attend memorial services, make casseroles, send cards and letters, and telephone. It calls us not to use our own busyness or ambivalence about death and grieving as excuses not to offer a compassionate response.

### Opening to New Revelation

Kisa Gotami seeks from the Buddha something that will bring her son back to life, something that will negate what has happened. She seeks to assuage her overwhelming grief by denying the reality of her beloved son's death. The Buddha gently sends her on an impossible mission to find mustard seed, which allows her to slowly grasp a deep understanding that she previously knew only in passing. "Kisa, don't you remember? My father died a year ago, and we were sad for a long time." It is when she sits down under the banyan tree that Kisa opens herself to new revelation. She cries until the crying stops. Finally, she understands that acceptance of death as part of the human condition will ease her suffering, and that the best response to this human suffering is to offer compassion to those who grieve.

### Finding Wisdom Through the Principles and Sources

This tale from the Buddhist tradition about the universality of grief acknowledges that one of the bonds that unite us as human beings is the experience of mourning. It reminds us that, no matter how much we may disagree about what happens after death, the experience of loss and grief is a universal one. The story invites us to be intentional about learning how to respond with compassion to the grief of others. It invites us to acknowledge our own humanity when our time of mourning is upon us.

## Connecting with Our Lives

### In Our Faith Communities

This story bears repeating. It can be a touchstone story for children, one that is so familiar that they can retell it themselves. As part of an annual All Souls' Sunday memorial service, it can help create space for children, youth, and families to acknowledge the presence of death in their lives and in the congregation. If you do choose to tell the story annually, involve children in helping. If the story is well known to the children, you can re-create conversations with Kisa Gotami's neighbors using volunteers to play the role of each neighbor. You might also pass around a dish of mustard seed, inviting each participant to hold a few grains as you tell the story.

The story lends itself to a conversation with children about what to do when someone they know is grieving. Offer age-appropriate suggestions about how to respond. Bring a number of sympathy cards and allow children to see how they look and what they say. Youth may find cards that express a theology they find problematic and provocative to consider and discuss. Tell children what generally happens at a memorial service or funeral in your congregation and at calling hours at a funeral home. Invite children to share any experiences they have had with funerals, memorial services, or wakes. Answer their questions to the best of your ability. Practice with them some words they might say to a friend whose grandparent has died. Make a sympathy card for someone in your congregation or for someone they know. The purpose of this activity and conversation is to help children develop understanding about customs and traditions that surround mourning, so that they are not frightened and confused if they are mourners themselves. It also gives them specific ways to respond with compassion to others.

### At Home

Responding with compassion to another's grief is a skill that can be taught. This story provides a way for families to begin a conversation about death and to acknowledge that it touches all people. Share stories of your own experiences with death, your first attendance at a funeral or memorial service or the death of someone you loved. Invite questions and reflections about Kisa Gotami's experience or the ones you have shared and guide children toward the understanding that every person and every family has their turn with the sadness of losing a loved one.

# Abu Kassim's Shoes

This story, drawn from original Persian and Arabic versions, will leave you and your listeners laughing as the troubles of a miserly merchant pile up. It is a preposterous tale about the consequences of being self-centered and tight-fisted. It invites us to consider the ways that we fail to be generous with loved ones and with the world at large. As we laugh at Abu Kassim and his troubles, we are gently prodded to consider our own fondness for material goods.

The story starts and ends with Abu Kassim's shoes, which symbolize his stinginess. When telling the tale, linger over the shoes, describing their patches and emphasizing how "heavy" the shoes are. Use a heavy, deep voice when you mention the shoes and allow your shoulders to sag and your body language to suggest being weighted down. Encourage listeners to join you in acting out this posture each time the shoes are mentioned.

"Abu Kassim's Shoes" is a cautionary tale, one that warns us against a particular kind of behavior, but it is not subtle. Children and adults alike will delight in imagining the absurd scenes as the tale unfolds, and they will easily grasp the message that comes at the conclusion as Abu Kassim is transformed by his experience and learns to engage in the world as a generous and responsible person.

ⓖ

Once there was a merchant who was known throughout Baghdad. He was a clever merchant, perhaps the richest in the city, but he was known everywhere for being a mean old miser. He never gave even one penny away, and his family lived in a house with no furniture and had only the poorest of clothing.

Abu Kassim's stinginess showed in the way he dressed. He wore a tattered and patched old robe and a headscarf that was so faded that no one could tell its original color. He was known most of all for his worn, patched shoes. He had had them for twenty years, never seeing the need to replace them when they wore out. He simply had the cobbler patch them until the shoes were just a mass of patches sewed on top of patches, and so heavy with all the extra leather that he could barely pick up his feet when he walked. When people heard his shuffling step, they said, "There goes Abu Kassim and his big heavy shoes. A tighter-fisted man we have never known!"

Now it came to pass one day that he had made an unusually good bargain. He had purchased some lovely jars at an excellent price and some nice perfume to fill them. Leaving the jars on his windowsill, he went off to celebrate by having a massage and a warm soak at the public bath.

When Abu Kassim came out of his bath, refreshed, he was amazed to find a brand-new pair of soft leather shoes in the place where his had been. Thinking that someone had made him a present, and muttering to himself about the stroke of luck that got him out of buying new shoes, he slipped on the brand-new pair and strode off down the road.

It was not long after that the chief judge of the town came out of the bath and looked for his new shoes. Instead, he found in the corner some tattered, patched, stinking old shoes. He knew instantly who had taken his brand-new shoes, and ordered that Abu Kassim be arrested and brought to court.

"Abu Kassim!" shouted the angry judge. "You stole my shoes and now you must pay a fine of five-hundred dinars or go to jail."

No matter how much Abu Kassim tried to explain that it was all a mistake, the judge would not listen. Abu Kassim left the court five hundred dinars poorer, carrying his heavy, tattered shoes by the laces.

On the way home from court, Abu Kassim threw the shoes into the Tigris River. It wasn't long after that when some fishermen downstream pulled on their net, thinking that they had an extraordinarily big fish. When the net finally surfaced, they saw that it held Abu Kassim's famous shoes. The nails from the shoes had ripped holes in the net that would require a full day to repair. Angrily, they took the shoes and threw them through Abu Kassim's window, smashing all his jars of expensive perfume. As Abu Kassim looked at the shoes sitting in the middle of a mess of broken glass and perfume, he resolved to get rid of them somehow.

He went outside to dig a hole and bury them. Now in the town of Baghdad, it was against the law to bury treasure. A neighbor who had never been fond of the tight-fisted man who lived next door reported to the authorities that Abu Kassim had buried treasure. The merchant found himself back before the same angry judge. "Fifty-thousand dinars fine this time! You will not break the law, you stingy old miser!"

On the way home from court, Abu Kassim cursed the heavy old shoes and threw them into an open sewage channel that took away the town's wastewater. "You belong with the sewage," he said to his shoes, flinging them away.

The shoes floated down the sewer pipes, from the larger pipes to the smaller, narrower ones. Eventually, they came to a stop, blocking the sewer pipe completely. The pipe filled with sewage, which backed up into the streets and into people's homes. When the workmen came to fix the problem, guess what they found? Abu Kassim's shoes blocking the pipe.

Back to court he went. "You and your shoes have damaged the whole town," the judge said. I order you to pay five-hundred thousand dinars for the clean-up!" Abu Kassim had to pay, but it took almost all the money that he had hoarded for all of his working life.

Abu Kassim, desperate, decided to burn his shoes. He set them outside on the second-floor porch to dry out so he could burn them. It wasn't long before a puppy came and started to play with them, dropping one onto the head of a passing woman and knocking her to the pavement.

"Enough," said Abu Kassim when the woman's husband hauled him back before the judge.

"You may have everything I own! But please," he said to the judge, "please write an order that allows me to disown any responsibility for what my shoes might do from now on." Trying hard not to smile, the judge agreed.

Abu Kassim was a different man after that. He paid attention to others, giving to the poor and helping his neighbors. He took proper care of his family's needs. And when his shoes wore out, he did not fail to buy himself a new pair!

## Meaning and Wisdom for Unitarian Universalists

### Hearing a Calling

This story calls us to share what we have and to engage with our families, our neighbors, and the world. Abu Kassim, weighted down by the impossibly patched old shoes, unable to keep himself and the shoes from damaging everything they touch, calls us to a renewed examination of our own behavior. Where in our lives might we be more generous and more engaged?

### Opening to New Revelation

Abu Kassim reminds us that money is for spending. It is not an end in itself but rather a means of creating and sustaining that which we value: our families, our communities, and our own lives. The merchant is seduced by money and is unable to part with it for even the most basic of items, a pair of shoes. His old shoes, symbols of his stinginess, are impossibly heavy. The shoes and his stinginess make it impossible for him to interact with his neighbors, his family, and the world. This story leads us to ask what prevents us from engaging more fully and more generously with the world around us? What damage is being done as a result? How can we renounce that which weights us down and invite a renewed spirit of generosity and engagement into our lives?

### Principles and Sources

The wisdom contained in this story is from the Islamic tradition. The other "character" in the story, the one that suffers damage from the merchant's lack of generosity and engagement, is the community at large. The shoes certainly afflict Abu Kassim, but the primary victims of those shoes and of Abu Kassim's stinginess are members of the community—his family, his neighbors, the fisherman, and ultimately the entire town. Abu Kassim is slow to learn that what is necessary in order to stop the ever-increasing damage is that he renounce his shoes and his tight-fistedness. The understanding we take from this tale is wisdom that Abu Kassim learns at a very high price. When we are weighted down with self-centered behavior, not engaged with our families, communities and the world, we suffer.

## Connecting with Our Lives

### In Our Faith Communities

This story begs for dramatization. Help children re-create Abu Kassim's shoes by adding patches and other weights to an old pair of shoes. Assign roles as members of Kassim's community—neighbors, court observers and judges, fishermen, merchants at the bazaar, and so on. Perform the story, and encourage children to invent more adventures for Abu Kassim and his shoes to add to the drama. Those who are musical could write a ballad telling the story of the shoes to accompany the play.

Use the story at the start of the congregation's stewardship drive as a way to address generosity. Point out that Abu Kassim's wrongdoing is in not taking part in the community. He hoards money and does not fulfill his responsibilities to his family, his neighbors, and those who are less fortunate. Invite children to consider what they are responsible for and to and to name those things. Make a large poster that lists all of the ways that children contribute to the wider world and are generous in spirit. Some examples may include social justice work, environmental steward-ship, and service projects

Emphasize the heaviness of Abu Kassim's shoes and his self-centeredness. Who is hurt by the shoes? Other people and the community itself are the ones who are hurt. It is when the com-munity demands retribution through fines that Abu Kassim suf-fers as well. Invite children to invent stories about someone who is hurt by another's stinginess. Record those stories on tape or act them out. Invented stories will allow children to share their own experiences in a nonthreatening way. Following the invented sto-ries, ask children how their stories would change if the people in-volved had been generous.

*At Home*

Have a good laugh over this story. Fully imagine all of the scenes in the story and all of the ways in which Abu Kassim's shoes get him into trouble. As a family, have a symbolic ceremony and discard your old shoes, inviting family members to each name a way in which they will be more generous as they discard their old shoes.

Talk with your family about the "weight" of Abu Kassim's shoes. Whom do the shoes hurt most? Who is hurt when we are stingy? Talk about the ways in which stinginess hurts both Abu Kassim and those in the community around him. Share with your family your own financial and volunteer commitments and the reasons why you make those commitments. To whom do you do-nate money and/or time and why? Which causes, organizations, or communities claim the largest portion of your gifts and why?

# The Call of Samuel

This story from the Hebrew Bible is about a young boy who grows up to be a prophet. It takes him time to hear and to accept his calling. He plays an important role in leading the Hebrew people at a crucial moment in their history. This story is about choices: How do we choose to respond when we are called to do something important or to make an important decision?

"The Call of Samuel" marks a transition in the story of the people of Israel. Arriving in the Promised Land after the Exodus from Egypt and the journey in the wilderness, they found themselves in need of some kind of government. The Philistines, who lived right along the coast, were pressuring them militarily, raiding and taking over villages. Against this backdrop, a boy named Samuel is born to a mother who was previously barren. She dedicates Samuel, her first-born, to the service of the Temple at Shiloh, which was at that time the center of Jewish worship. While Samuel is sleeping one night, God wakes him, calling his name three separate times before Samuel "gets it" and listens to what God has to say: He is to be a prophet and wise person among his people. Many years later, Samuel is called to anoint the first king of Israel, changing the loose confederation style of government into a centralized monarchy.

The story that follows is an easy one to tell. It resonates with children and adults alike. Who among us has not had the experience of being awakened from sleep by something important? Who has not experienced repeated calls to wake up? Who has not had the experience of not understanding what we are being asked to do? Enlist listeners' help calling Samuel's name, over and over again.

Once there was a woman named Hannah, a young wife who was unable to have a child. Deeply saddened by this, she went each year to the Temple at Shiloh, where the Ark of the Covenant, the Throne of God, rested. There she offered sacrifice and prayed for the birth of a child. One year, Eli, the high priest at the temple, overheard her tearful prayer. He heard her promise that if she had a son, she would give him over to the Temple to be trained in the ways of a priest. It was not long after that she conceived and in due course bore a son, calling him Samuel. When the child was three years old, she brought him to the Temple at Shiloh and gave him into the care and nurture of Eli, promising to return each year to visit the child.

After Samuel came to live at the Temple at Shiloh, he quickly became very useful to Eli, whose eyesight was failing. Samuel fetched things for Eli, whom he loved, and cleaned and cared for the Temple. Samuel's biggest and most important job was to sleep each night near the Ark of the Covenant, making sure that it was well guarded and that the candles on a seven-branched candle stand near it never burned out. Each night as Eli slept in his sleeping room, Samuel lay on his mat, sleeping lightly, guarding the Ark, listening in case Eli needed him.

One night, there came a voice: "Samuel! Samuel!"

Responding, "Here I am," Samuel went to Eli to ask what the high priest needed.

"I did not call you," said Eli. "Go back and lie down."

Samuel returned to his mat, only to hear again: "Samuel! Samuel!" Again he went to Eli and again Eli told him that he had not called.

Samuel then heard the voice for the third time: "Samuel! Samuel!" He ran to Eli.

The high priest knew that it was God who was calling to Samuel. He told Samuel to respond the next time, saying, "Speak, for your servant is listening."

Samuel did as he was told. The next time the voice called, Samuel said, "Speak, for your servant is listening!" and God spoke to Samuel. God told him that he was to be a prophet, that he would speak for all that was good and right and true, and that the people of Israel would look to him for wisdom and understanding.

Samuel grew in stature and wisdom, becoming the prophet he had been called to be. He advised and guided the people of Israel as they struggled against the Philistine enemy, who battled with war chariots, weapons of iron, and military power that Samuel's people could not match. He helped them pay attention not just to warring but also to how they treated one another and to what kind of people they were going to be.

Over time, the people of Israel came to believe that they needed a strong warrior leader, a king who would build an army. The elders gathered together and came to Samuel, now an old man, and begged him to appoint a king to govern them who would be a strong leader and commander. Samuel argued that having a king was not such a good idea. A king would take their sons and make them fight wars. A king would demand riches and require servants to plow and plant his land. He would take their daughters as cooks and bakers and perfumers. He would take the best of the vineyards and olive orchards and give them to his friends. No matter how much Samuel argued against it, the elders of Israel still believed that a strong king was the only answer to the threat from the Philistines. Reluctantly, the prophet Samuel anointed Saul to be king of all Israel and to gather an army to fight the Philistines.

Samuel remained a wise counselor and advisor to the new king, speaking on behalf of what was good and right and true for the rest of his days.

ⓖ

## Meaning and Wisdom for Unitarian Universalists

### Hearing a Calling

We have all at one time or another experienced a call to take on a major challenge or to make a significant change in our own lives and work. In the story, the call to become a prophet comes quietly but persistently. It wakes Samuel from his sleep and demands that he pay attention to it. How do we respond when we perceive that there is something in our own lives or in the world that needs attention and requires a response? The wisdom in this story from the Hebrew tradition reminds us that an important call will not be ignored. We cannot simply "go back to sleep" once we perceive that there is something we are called to do in the world.

### Opening to New Revelation

Samuel is asleep when the call first comes. It wakes him up, not once but three times. It is Eli who understands that Samuel must open himself to new revelation, new insight, and a new challenge. Samuel's choice to respond by opening his heart and mind invites us to make the same choice, waking up to that which we are called to do in the world.

### Finding Wisdom Through the Principles and Sources

It is a sacred responsibility to be called to speak and act on behalf of that which is good and right and true. This story from the Jewish tradition invites us to acknowledge that sacredness of a call to justice making or service. Our own calls to service are ways of carrying our Unitarian Universalist faith into the world.

The conversation between Samuel and the elders of Israel about how to address the threat to their people offers wisdom pertinent to us now. Samuel clearly points out the dangers of establishing a more powerful government; the elders fear enslavement by the Philistines. There is potential peril either way. This age-old conversation centers on infringement of civil liberties in the name of security, a topic for modern times as well.

## Connecting with Our Lives

*In Our Faith Communities*

This story is wonderful to act out with children, who often have their own experiences of being called and not wanting to answer. Ask each child in turn to act like Samuel while the rest of the group calls the child's name, so that each has the experience of being called three times before understanding the source of the call.

Engage children and adults in conversation about prophets. In the Unitarian Universalist tradition, each of us can be a prophet, speaking and acting for what is good and right and true. Ask them to name some modern-day prophets. Find a cloak or scarf and imagine with children that it is a prophet's mantle. Invite children to take turns wearing it and naming something they will do in their own lives to serve this faith. Point out that simple acts such as picking up litter or caring for others are prophetic acts.

*At Home*

A compelling part of the story is that even as a child Samuel has very important tasks at the Temple at Shiloh. Discuss the important tasks or roles children hold in a family. Adults can share their own childhood stories as well. Explore the callings and contributions children make in your family today. Are there important tasks that can be given to children in your family? How, as a family, do you contribute to the values of Unitarian Universalist faith? Although we envision prophets as individuals, families can contribute together to the unfolding of faith.

# Easter

This story is from the Christian Bible. It tells of the last days of Jesus of Nazareth and what happened after his death. This version includes the open tomb and emphasizes how Jesus' followers came to terms with his death at the hands of the Roman Empire. It is a story of the triumph of hope and love over despair, cruelty, and death.

The story of Jesus of Nazareth's death and resurrection is surrounded by many layers of theology, church history, and church tradition. The rendition that follows is the story of a prophet executed by an empire that valued the order of the Pax Romana above all else and used torture and execution to enforce that order. It is a story about followers and friends whose fear and despair were cast aside as they experienced the enduring power of Jesus' message. It is a story of rebirth and transformation that offers to Unitarian Universalists a way to understand and embrace this central Christian narrative.

In the days when Pontius Pilate, the Roman Procurator, ruled all of Palestine with great cruelty, there lived a Jewish prophet and teacher named Jesus of Nazareth. Jesus moved from place to place, offering hope to people who desperately needed reason to hope. He taught that every single person is loved by God, and that there is a place for everyone in the Kingdom of Heaven. He reached out to all kinds of people, including those who were hated or ignored by others: poor people, sick people, women without husbands, and tax collectors.

Large crowds gathered around to hear Jesus' message of hope, love, and welcome. This made Pontius Pilate and the Romans worry that he was a dangerous troublemaker. There came a time when Jesus decided to go Jerusalem, the big city, to challenge those in power by saying that all people were loved and worthwhile. It was a dangerous thing to do, but his message needed to be heard. On Thursday night of the week he entered Jerusalem, he shared a meal with his friends and went with them to the Garden of Gethsemane to pray for strength and courage. There he was arrested by Roman soldiers.

The next day, Jesus was sentenced to die a cruel death by being nailed to a wooden cross, which was the Roman punishment for people considered troublemakers. On the Friday that he was put to death, his friends all scattered, frightened that the Roman soldiers would hurt them too.

After Jesus' death, a follower named Joseph of Arimathea took his body and washed and prepared it for burial. He placed Jesus's body in a tomb and rolled a heavy stone across the entrance.

Jesus' supporters were sad beyond all words and terribly afraid. They felt hopeless. The messenger of hope was gone from them, crushed and killed by the cruel Roman Empire. What were they to do?

On the third day after Jesus' death, three women went to the place where Jesus was buried, bringing spices to anoint his body. On the way, they talked about how difficult it would be to roll away the heavy stone in front of the tomb. When they got there, they found the stone rolled away and Jesus' body gone! The women ran from that place, frightened.

Not long after that, Jesus' friends and supporters began to talk with one another about his teachings. They thought about his message of hope and his belief that each and every one of us is loved by God. They heard the reports from the women about the empty tomb. They wondered. Sometimes when they talked about the things Jesus had said, it seemed like he was right there with them. So strong was his presence that many followers said that Jesus had returned as a holy spirit. They said, as Christians do today, that Jesus was born again, or resurrected.

They remembered the love Jesus taught and gradually they began to feel hope again. Their sadness didn't go away completely, but it faded. As they remembered Jesus, they knew deep in their hearts that love is stronger than cruelty and stronger than death. His spirit lived on as it does today.

## Meaning and Wisdom for Unitarian Universalists

### Hearing a Calling

The Easter story of Jesus of Nazareth's death and resurrection calls us to renewed hope. Jesus' followers have reason to believe that all is lost and they scatter, nursing their wounded spirits, but three women refuse to succumb to despair. At the tomb, in the face of death itself, the women find hope in the form of a rolled-away stone. Death and cruelty are not the final chapter of the story, as love and hope triumph and the spirit and message of their beloved prophet live on.

### Opening to New Revelation

This is a story usually told in the springtime, as the natural world is reborn. Dormant, seemingly dead plants set forth new shoots. Baby birds are born. The days grow longer and warmer. As we hear this story anew, it reveals an ancient truth and wisdom, echoed in the natural world and in the resilience of the human spirit: Even in the most trying of times, transformation is possible.

### Finding Wisdom Through the Principles and Sources

Unitarian Universalist tradition has its roots in the Christian tradition. Many Unitarian Universalists view Jesus as a teacher and a prophet and are skeptical of the Biblical story that includes physical resurrection. Whatever one's views about its literal truth, the story of Jesus of Nazareth's death and resurrection—a central story in the Christian tradition—has important wisdom for all of us. It offers a life-affirming message of hope and love, an antidote to despair even in the most difficult of times.

This version of the story places the blame for the crucifixion of Jesus squarely on the shoulders of the Roman government, whose cruel means of dealing with troublemakers is well documented. Because Western literature, theology, and tradition have a long and dangerous history of blaming Jewish people for the death of Jesus, it is important to present to children and adults a picture and telling that refute that charge.

## Connecting with Our Lives

### In Our Faith Communities

This story is one that children have likely heard from other sources, which makes it imperative to share the story from a Unitarian Universalist point of view. Retell the Easter story, stopping as necessary to answer children's questions. Be prepared to answer theological questions directly and to share your own views about the story. Guide children away from dwelling on the cruelty of Jesus' death, emphasizing instead the feelings of his friends and followers as they move from hope at hearing his message, to despair after his death, to a renewed hope as they realize that the message of love did not die.

Go outside and look for signs of rebirth in the natural world. Send children on a hunt to find new life in the midst of what looks dead; new sprouts in the midst of last year's dead foliage or under last year's leaves are examples. Invite children to consider how their discoveries in the natural world are similar to the Easter story of renewal.

### At Home

Share with your family your own understanding of this story and what it means. Answer any questions, focusing the conversation on the message of hope and love. Children may want to talk more about Christian views of this story. Their increased understanding of different views of the Easter story and resurrection will help them come to their own conclusions. Explain different points of view in a way that models respect for others' beliefs even when you disagree with them. Emphasize that Jesus' teachings were so prophetic and aligned with many common religious values that they have been kept alive for centuries.

If your family has a garden, search for signs of spring, especially new growth coming from that which has died. Going further afield, search for dead tree or stumps that have given rise to new forms of life. Point out the parallel between the message of the Easter story and their discovery that life can begin again even in the presence of death.

# Charles Darwin

Charles Darwin was a great collector of beetles, rocks, and other natural things as a child. Born to a wealthy family with Unitarian connections, he tried his hand at the study of both medicine and ministry, but did not find his true calling as a naturalist until he studied botany and zoology. He traveled around the world discovering uniquely adapted species in South America, most famously on the Galapagos Islands off Ecuador. Darwin's broad background in botany, zoology, paleontology, and geology enabled him to piece together the mystery of how each species emerges and becomes differentiated from others.

The idea of evolution was not new with Charles Darwin: His grandfather Erasmus Darwin proposed the idea that all creatures on earth share a common ancestor. Charles Darwin's contribution was the idea that natural selection is the means by which evolution happens. A methodical scientist, Darwin spent twenty-two years after the voyage developing his theory of evolution by natural selection. It was published in 1859 in *The Origin of Species*, a book that shook the Western world.

Both of Darwin's grandfathers, Josiah Wedgwood and Erasmus Darwin, were freethinkers and Unitarians, as was his mother, Susannah. Charles was a religious skeptic, which caused a great deal of sadness for his wife, Emma. When his ten-year-old daughter died, he lost all faith in Christianity, preferring to take a walk rather than attend church on Sundays. His sense of wonder about the world and his quest for revelation through direct observation remained. These traits, likely nurtured by his Unitarian heritage, make him an important figure in our faith tradition.

The following story focuses on Darwin discovering his true calling. His irrepressible curiosity about the world around him led him to develop skills in the natural sciences that had both breadth and depth. His broad understanding of the natural world enabled the leap in imagination that led to the development of his ideas about natural selection. This story speaks to the naturalist in all of us.

From the time he was a little boy, Charles Darwin was an explorer. He loved to roam the fields and hills near his home in Shrewsbury, England. He was fascinated by the movements of small animals and insects and knew each wildflower by name. He was curious about everything he saw and heard and touched, wondering at the lives of ants and butterflies, examining and collecting rocks, delighting in the grasses, trees, leaves, and flowers that provided homes for his very favorite creature—the beetle.

Curiosity about the world and the place of humans in it was a gift given to Charles by both his grandfathers. They were Unitarians and believed that human beings did not yet know all the answers to life's great questions. The clues were to be found in observing the world around them.

When Charles was eight, his mother died. Not long after, his father decided to send Charles away to school, where he might learn the things that young gentlemen in his day were expected to know: Greek, Latin, and ancient history. But Charles was more interested in the workings of an anthill or the mysteries found in a rock pile than he was in what was taught at school. At every opportunity he took long walks outdoors, watching, listening, and collecting. He delighted in figuring out how creatures behaved and how the natural world worked.

This wasn't at all what Charles's father had in mind. He was worried. What would young Charles do when he grew up? What kind of man would he be?

When Charles was fifteen, his father sent him to medical school to become a doctor like his father and grandfather. But he was not interested in medicine. Instead, he found people who would teach him all about different kinds of plants. He began to draw these plants in great detail, labeling all the parts, learning to tell one variety from another.

Two years later, Charles left medical school; it was clear that he didn't want to be a doctor. His father was furious and thought that the endless hours Charles spent outdoors were a waste of time. Determined that Charles would make something of himself, his father sent him to Cambridge University to become a minister.

Charles was not unhappy with that decision; in those days, ministers often did science experiments and observations in their spare time. Charles planned to find a small church in the countryside and spend most of his time observing and drawing plants, animals, rocks, and insects.

He was still very interested in collecting beetles. One day, Charles tore a piece of bark off a tree and saw two rare kinds of beetles. He had one in each hand when he saw a third that he wanted to add to his collection. He quickly popped one beetle into his mouth in order to grab the third—with very bad results. The beetle squirted something nasty-tasting and Charles was forced to spit it out.

At Cambridge, Charles discovered what his life's work would be and began to call himself a naturalist. When he was nineteen, he was invited to spend five years traveling around the world on the HMS Beagle, serving as its naturalist. His job was to draw and make notes on plants, animals, and rock formations everywhere the ship went. With some strong support from his Uncle Josiah, Charles was eventually able to convince his father that this proposed journey was a good idea. On December 27, 1831, he left on a five-year voyage that would change his understanding of the world. On that trip, he began to piece together clues to the great puzzle then called "the mystery of mysteries," how all of the different forms of life on earth came to be.

As he traveled, Charles filled notebooks with drawings and notes. He stayed open to the curiosities of the natural world as they presented themselves: frogs, salamanders, armadillos, insects, and lots of fossils. When he returned to England five years later, he understood how plants and animals evolved from one form to another over the course of many, many thousands and millions of years.

Twenty-two years later Charles finally published *The Origin of Species*. Scientists, preachers, and teachers took notice, and so did the press. The boy collector with the gift of wonder, a spirit of adventure, and openness to new ideas had become the scientist whose theory responded to the "mystery of mysteries." Today, people still take notice and debate what Charles Darwin had to say.

## Meaning and Wisdom for Unitarian Universalists

### Hearing a Calling

From a very early age, Darwin was called to make his contribution to the world through his gift for the natural sciences and his love for observation and experimentation. He needed to be outdoors, attentively observing nature. He sought out teachers and experiences that prepared him to respond to the opportunity to be a naturalist when it presented itself. Our Unitarian Universalist faith calls upon each of us to figure out how our own gifts and skills can help make the world a better place.

### Opening to New Revelation

Darwin was curious and thoughtful, observing sometimes for hours on end, trying to tease out an understanding of what he was seeing. He drew on the various disciplines with which he was familiar (botany, zoology, paleontology, and geology) to help him recognize new possibilities and be open to new revelation. Believing that revelation is continuous rather than complete, Unitarian Universalists seek always to discover deeper truth and meaning in our lives and in our experience of the world.

## Finding Wisdom Through the Principles and Sources

"Direct experience of transcending mystery and wonder" is one of the Sources of our faith tradition. Darwin brought not only solid scientific technique to his work, but also a passionate curiosity and wonder that pushed him toward new discoveries.

## Connecting with Our Lives

### In Our Faith Communities

This story might well be told at a time of the year when children and families are engaged in outdoor exploration, collecting rocks, identifying birds, or finding wildflowers. Invite children to share their collections of natural items. Children and families might want to share stories of a time when they paid attention to something for a long time (e.g., a small stream, a bug on water, a chipmunk, an ant hill). What did they discover? What wisdom did they learn by taking the time to observe? Be sure to broaden your definition of paying attention to include hearing and touching as well as seeing.

You might want to go on a "paying attention" excursion. Take a walk and invite children to find something in the natural world to really notice for a period of time. As a group, share what children have observed. Invite them to ponder with gratitude all that they love about nature and the outdoors. Next have each person name all the things about creation they notice and are grateful for: Waterfalls, aardvarks, ladybugs, and brightly colored leaves are some possibilities. Compose a litany of thanks from the lists. Share it as part of a Thanksgiving service, honoring the abundance all around.

*At Home*

As a family, spend time in wonder at the marvels of creation in its myriad forms. Honoring our naturalist spirit nurtures an ethic of gratitude. As part of mealtime blessing or chalice lighting, include mention of all that family members notice in the natural world. Explore the idea of "calling" with children. Are there passions that call them as Darwin was called to his work as a naturalist? Discuss their visions, dreams, and callings.

# Sand

This story is far more ancient than the oldest of wisdom stories told by human beings. It is a wisdom story about the very earth we inhabit. It is the story of our earth and its evolution over millions and billions of years.

Stories of science contain both facts and spiritual wisdom. When we convey scientific knowledge as a story, we link it to our everyday lives, and we are able to touch the spirit as well as the intellect. Sand, familiar to all of us, offers a story that tells of the wonder and vastness of the history of our earth. This commonplace substance becomes extraordinary.

Before telling this story, invite the listener to carefully examine a sample of sand, touching it and looking closely at its composition. Help the listeners to think of the many places where sand is found, and to wonder at how it got there. As you tell the story, linger over the numbers of years, inviting all to contemplate just how old our beloved earth is. Enter the story and the contemplation of sand in a spirit of discovery. Let it lead to more wondering and more questions.

Did you know that scientists have figured out that there are more than seven quintillion five quadrillion grains of sand on our earth? That is seven followed by five and then seventeen zeroes. There has been sand on our earth for more than three hundred million years, and here is its story.

Six hundred million years ago, the earth was still cooling from its birth explosion billions of years earlier. At that time all life was found in the warm oceans, and there was a lot of it. Many new kinds of life had evolved in a relatively short period of time. The earth we know today looked much different. The land that is now North America was actually south of the equator. It had a shallow, warm ocean covering about two-thirds of what is now the United States, Canada, and Mexico.

The water had something called calcium carbonate in it, which is the lime we might spread on our gardens to help feed our plants. The early bacteria and small plants in the warm ocean learned over time how to gather this lime from the water. Over the course of many millions of years, animals evolved that had external shells and protective coverings made out of the lime taken from the water. When they died, their shells fell to the ocean floor, making a thick mass.

About three hundred million years ago, things changed. The sea that had covered most of what is now North America drained. It formed the Atlantic Ocean, leaving behind great deposits of limestone. At the same time, earthquakes and volcanoes caused great mineral mountains to rise in both the east (the Appalachians) and the west (the Rockies).

Sand began to form when tiny pieces of mountain broke off or were worn off by the action of rain, wind, or plant life. Those tiny pieces were washed by rainwater into small streams making their way down the mountain. They bounced and rolled along, their surface getting worn by rubbing against other small grains, or against the water. At times, the sand grains rested, possibly for thousands of years, behind a boulder or in some other protected place. Eventually, the grains made it to a big river or to the ocean itself, but it took a long time; in a million years, a grain of sand moved only one hundred miles downstream. When the streams or rivers moved across land that had once been the warm ocean, the leftover lime deposits dissolved into the water again. These grains of sand mixed with sand from the mountains, moving, churning, and heading toward the sea.

About one hundred and ninety million years ago, there was a great river that started in the Appalachian Mountains and moved sand westward across the North American continent. It left great deposits of sand in what is now the midwestern part of the continent. Sand traveled by river from the eastern part of the United States and landed in places like Utah.

When the sand, a mixture of grains of mountain and tiny bits of limestone, reached the ocean, it mixed with tiny leftover pieces of life from the ocean itself to form beaches. Each beach is different, depending on the combination of mountain grains and leftover bits of dead sea creatures. When the most recent of earth's twenty ice ages ended, the glaciers melted back from the northern part of North America. That was one hundred and eighty thousand years ago. The melting ice left behind more remains of once-living creatures that became part of the mixture we know as sand.

Across all the years, sand has not stopped moving. With every wave and every gust of wind, sand is taken up into the ocean or into the air, only to mix with whatever else is in the water or air. The sand comes down someplace else. It can end up in our sand castles, or under our feet, or in our favorite pails.

That is the story of sand, as ancient as the mountains of our earth, and containing parts of life forms millions of years old. Always changing, it is a witness to the unfolding of earth's story.

ⓖ

## Meaning and Wisdom for Unitarian Universalists

*Hearing a Calling*
Locating ourselves in the context of earth's great unfolding opens us to a spiritual depth beyond the everyday. Knowing that we share space with tiny sand grains that have been witnesses to millions of years of history affirms our connection to this earth. It invites us to a renewed commitment to care for our shared home on this planet and deepens our respect for that which we often take for granted. It calls us to gratitude for the interdependent web to which we belong.

*Opening to New Revelation*
Often we go through life focused on what we are doing next, our families, schoolwork, our jobs, and tomorrow's schedule. This story invites us to stop and contemplate our lives and the vastness of time. Taking time to imagine our continent nearly covered in a warm ocean incubating life, or hosting a great river flowing and bringing sand from the eastern mountain range to what is now our western desert area, allows us to feel both the smallness of our own lives and the greatness of the earth of which we are part.

*Finding Wisdom Through the Principles and Sources*
Unitarian Universalists embrace the guidance and teachings of science as part of our tradition. We delight in scientific discoveries that enhance our understanding of the world in which we live. Weaving science into story form helps us better grasp its concepts. It also unveils how the teachings of science can offer ethical, moral, and spiritual guidance to help us live more fully.

## Connecting with Our Lives

*In Our Faith Communities*
This story can be explored in many different ways. Children may want to learn more about sand. Inexpensive magnifying glasses

and microscopes will reveal the complexities of each grain. A field trip to a beach, lakeshore, or desert area can help children contemplate just how many grains of sand there are in the world. Members of the congregation who are scientists or geologists—amateur or professional—can be invited to share some of their knowledge and specialized equipment. Small quantities of sand can be used for art projects, such as sand paintings or landscapes of beaches or deserts, using actual sand glued to the picture.

## At Home

Start a sand collection with your family. Gather and label a small sample from each place your family visits. Pay attention to the omnipresence of sand, watching for it in running water and in the wind. Look at sand under a microscope and learn something about it through Internet research. Introduce your family to some of the current uses for sand; glass, silicon wafers for computer chips, and water filtering are examples.

Engage your family in the study of prehistoric earth, learning about its geological features and their changes over time. How does knowing about and appreciating the long history of earth make us better people? What actions will we take to reflect our gratitude for the earth? Make a family plan to be better earth citizens, and carry it out.

# Nanabush and the Bulrushes

This is a story from the Anishinabe Nation. The Anishinabe (Ojibway) people come primarily from the area around the Great Lakes, especially Lake Superior, in the states of Wisconsin, Minnesota, and Michigan and in the Canadian province of Ontario. One of the traditional ways in which cultural values are taught is through the adventures of a being called Nanabush. Part spirit and part human, Nanabush is clever, curious, compassionate, and well meaning. He is also impulsive, impatient, forgetful, and occasionally arrogant. He sometimes gets into sticky situations because he does not think before he acts, and he does not always follow instructions. His adventures are told as stories that teach human beings how to live better. He is sometimes the hero who bests an opponent through wit, speed, and daring, and sometimes the egoist whose pride leads to unpleasant consequences. Nanabush is beloved among the Anishinabe because he embodies the combination of qualities, both good and bad, that reflects their own experience of what it means to be human.

In this tale about showing off, the hero challenges others, trying to prove his superiority. It is only after many exhausting days of dancing that he discovers that he has foolishly challenged the marsh bulrushes to a dancing contest. In telling the story, emphasize the hunger and the weariness of Nanabush as he keeps dancing. What starts out as fun goes on and on for him. Keep the ending a surprise until the last moment.

If your listeners are not likely to have seen or to know about bulrushes or cattails, bring samples or pictures from the Internet to show them. Invite them to imagine a dense stand of the plants swaying in the wind, looking like dancers.

This is a story told by the Anishinabe people who come from the area around Lake Superior, in Ontario, Wisconsin, Minnesota, and Michigan. It is a story about a hero, part human, and part spirit, called Nanabush.

At dusk, Nanabush was walking when he heard a sound. It was coming from the marshy place where the brook flowed into a pond. Nanabush approached and saw a great group of men dancing, swaying back and forth, nearly touching the ground. They had feathers perched upon their heads as they danced.

Nanabush loved to dance! He asked the swaying men if he could join them. The wind was strong, and in it he heard a reply: "Halloo … Halloo. Eight days we will dance."

Before Nanabush thought much about it, he said, "I can dance longer and better than you. I will still be dancing long after you are tired." No one answered his challenge, so Nanabush began to dance.

Nanabush danced and danced, happily moving and swaying, keeping up with the other dancers. When morning came, they were still dancing, and so was he. Another day and night of dancing went by, and another, and another.

By the end of the fourth day, Nanabush was feeling tired, but he had challenged those dancing men, and so he continued to dance. He danced and danced, showing off his very best technique, swaying and moving faster, then slower. He reached for the sky, and then he reached for the earth. It was a beautiful dance!

At seven days, he grew hungry. He wondered if he could keep up the dancing without first finding something to eat. But he kept on dancing through the day and into the night. He was weary beyond all description. He was anxious for the morning of the eighth day to come and for the dancing to stop, but sunrise was still a far way off. He was hungry, so hungry that he felt weak. And tired, so tired that there were tears in his eyes. And yet he kept going because he wanted to show that he was a better dancer than all the others.

At daybreak on the eighth day, Nanabush lay down, exhausted. The dance was over. The wind was dying down as well. As Nanabush lay on the ground, tired and hungry, he slowly became aware that his fellow dancers were not people at all, but tall marsh grasses and cattails. He had danced himself to exhaustion trying to keep up with bulrushes swaying in the wind.

## Meaning and Wisdom for Unitarian Universalists

### Hearing a Calling

This wisdom tale calls us to reexamine how we spend our time. Do we make choices based on what we are called to do? Do we spend time trying to outshine others? This tale reminds us to look carefully at situations when we are making choices. How often do we do something to excess, even something we love? When our lives feel like a frantic dance, our bodies sometimes call us to pace ourselves more evenly. Nanabush's experience offers us a cautionary tale for overscheduled lives.

### Opening to New Revelation

This story reminds us that our own competitiveness may keep us from assessing a situation accurately, which may cause us to act foolishly. Nanabush loves to dance and is clearly a good dancer, but his desire to outshine others leads him to continue to the point of exhaustion and hunger, to the point where dancing is no longer fun and he wants it to be over. The voice in the wind leads him to imagine that the dance will last for an excessively long eight days, too

much of a good thing. We, too, may take on more than we can han-
dle and find ourselves trapped in absurd and foolish situations.

### Finding Wisdom Through the Principles and Sources

Earth-centered traditions are sources of wisdom for Unitarian
Universalist faith. The teachers in this tale, the bulrushes and the
wind, are of the natural world. Had Nanabush listened more carefully to them at the start he would have been spared his exhaustion. The tale reminds us that time spent honoring and respecting
nature is ultimately time spent honoring and caring for ourselves.

## Connecting with Our Lives

### In Our Faith Communities

Take a field trip to a local marsh to see an expanse of bulrushes and
cattails, or look at pictures. Invite children to pretend they are bulrushes swaying in the wind, varying the wind from gentle to strong,
unidirectional to swirling, steady to gusty. Together, compose a wind
song and choreograph a bulrush dance to perform. Some children
may dance and others can provide the noise of the wind.

How does Nanabush feel when he discovers that he has been
competing against dancing bulrushes? Engage children in conversation about times when they have boasted about being better at
something than others. What was the result of the boasting? Make
a list together of the ways they compete with others and the ways
they cooperate with others. Are there times when competing is not
a good idea? Are there times when cooperating is not a good idea?

This story comes from the wisdom of the Anishinabe (Ojibway) people. Find out about the presence of Native American/First
Nation people in your geographical area. Are there people in your
faith community whose heritage is Native American? Is there wisdom from their heritage that they are willing to share with the
congregation?

*At Home*

With your family, share stories of when you have done something foolish and what lesson you learned from it. Have there been times when pride or competitiveness led you to make unwise choices? Share stories of your mistakes with your children. They will delight in knowing you have erred and learn about how we try our best, sometimes make mistakes, learn, and move on.

Learn about the Native American/First Nation people who live in your geographical area at present. Find children's books and wisdom stories written by those of that heritage and tradition. Become familiar with Oyate, an organization that publishes and reviews books about Native Americans, particularly those for children (www.oyate.org).

Take a canoe trip, a walk, or a car trip to view an expanse of bulrushes and cattails. If you are able, gather some to arrange in a vase. After seeing the plants dance in the wind, make up a family dance, pretending to be bulrushes in the wind.

# The Green Man

The natural world is full of mystery. Many Unitarian Universalists have pondered the natural world as a means to considering the greatness of life. Henry David Thoreau and Ralph Waldo Emerson wrote extensively about finding religion in nature. The beauty, order, and mystery in nature call us to consider our place on this shared earth.

Earth-centered traditions have long recognized and honored the power of nature. Ancients viewed the trees and the forest as divine. They honored the mystery of life's cycles—vegetation dying each autumn and rebirthing each spring. Pagan traditions have rituals and observances that bespeak a deep appreciation of nature. The fertility of the natural world, so crucial to the survival of life, then as now, is symbolized in the union of the Great Mother and her consort, the divine spirit of the trees. Christianity spread throughout Europe during the Middle Ages and the church assimilated many ancient pagan traditions. The various names for the Great Mother became the names of saints. Her male consort became the Tree of Life in Christian iconology. The Christian church saw the spirit of nature as reflecting God's grace.

The nature spirit figure persisted in the popular imagination and in folk literature. By the thirteenth century, it took the form of the Green Man, a head surrounded by leaves. This symbol of the natural world and our human connection to it is present in stonework on medieval cathedrals, in manuscripts of early Christian monks, on door signs, in castle artwork, and in public spaces throughout Europe. He appears in literary works as a man dressed in green who lives in the woods, one who is able to interpret and represent the natural world. Many familiar characters from literature seem based on the Green Man archetype—the Green Knight of Arthurian legend, Shakespeare's Puck, and Robin Hood. He persists in the popular imagination and today many gardeners and environmentalists adopt the figure as a symbol of the untamed and unfettered natural world.

There is speculation about the life and origin of the Green Man. If there is a nature spirit, where did it come from? Where exactly does it live? In this story, a rich young man finds himself spending a year alone in the woods, learning the lessons nature has to teach. The listener travels the same path as the young man, unsure what will happen next. The story evokes a sense of wonder and unveils the unpredictable transformation sometimes offered in life journeys.

The story that follows is an abridgment of Gail E. Haley's interpretive tale.

Once upon a time, there lived a rich and vain young squire. Servants prepared his favorite foods each day. His every wish was granted.

One of the young man's favorite things to do was to ride through the woods that were part of his kingdom, hunting small animals for sport. He thought that the woods and all its creatures belonged to him and he could do as he pleased with them.

The people in the village had a different idea about the woods. The woods provided a home to all the creatures that lived there: chipmunks, birds, squirrels, rabbits, deer, and wild pigs. They told their children a story about a Green Man who lived in the woods and cared for all of the small creatures. They said he even watched out for children in the woods. The villagers faithfully left out food on winter nights for the Green Man to eat.

One autumn day, the squire decided to go on a hunt. He called to all of his servants to saddle up the horses and get on their riding clothes: they were going into *his* woods.

They rode into the woods, trampling nests and dens as they went, sending dogs out ahead to chase small animals out of their homes so they could be easily hunted. After a time, the squire became separated from the rest of the hunting party. He was looking for them when he came to a pond—a beautiful, clear, cool pond. "How clever of me to have a pond in my woods to refresh myself!" he said.

The young man began to remove all of his fine clothing— his shoes, his hat, his jacket, his shirt, his pants, and his socks. He laid his clothes neatly folded by the edge of the pond and jumped into the cool water. He swam back and forth, enjoying himself immensely.

While he was swimming and splashing away, a hand reached out from behind a tree and took his clothing and led his horse away. When the squire got out of the water, he discovered that he had nothing left to wear save a piece of rope. He took the rope and fastened some leaves to it to make a cover up. When his hunting party came looking for him, he was embarrassed to be seen dressed in nothing but leaves, so he hid.

At night, the squire went looking for some shelter and he stumbled into a cave. He didn't sleep much that night. It was dark, and he was frightened, and he kept hearing animal noises all night.

In the morning, when the daylight came, he saw that he was not alone in the cave. There was a goat there, and a chicken, and a gourd for holding water. Someone had been living in that cave! He found some grass for the goat and feed for the chicken. He discovered some grain that he could eat as well.

Over time, the squire settled in to life in the cave. He fashioned a whole garment out of leaves. He ate eggs from the hen and drank milk from the goat. He covered his hand with mud to prevent stings and reached into a beehive for honey to eat. He became acquainted with all the small woodland creatures, and he cared for them, helping them over swollen streams when heavy rains fell, making sure they had food and water, and sheltering them in the cave on the chilly nights.

One day he came upon two small children trapped by a wild pig threatening to bite. When he had chased the pig off, they looked at him. There he was, covered head to toe with leaves and mud, with a wild-looking beard and hair. "Are you the Green Man?" they asked.

"I guess I am," said the man, who no longer looked anything like a squire.

When winter came, the Green Man was happy to go into the village at night and to take the food that the villagers left out for him, sharing it with all his animal friends.

A year passed peacefully, until one warm day when a hunting party came into the woods. The Green Man hid behind a tree to watch. A rich young man, a squire perhaps, became separated from his hunting group and decided to take a swim in the clear, cool pond. He took off his clothes, folded them, and left them under a tree. The Green Man reached out a hand and took the clothes and the horse, leaving behind his garment of leaves and a coil of rope. He used a sharp stick to trim his hair and beard, and rode into town, back to his parents' castle.

When he arrived, his parents were overjoyed to see him. But there was something different about the squire. After his time in the woods, he no longer wanted to hunt for sport. He had become a friend to all creatures of the wild.

In the winter, he never failed to leave out food for the Green Man.

## Meaning and Wisdom for Unitarian Universalists

### Hearing a Calling

As this tale begins, a privileged young squire treats the natural world as his dominion, to be used solely for his own pleasure and purposes. In the course of the story, he learns to live in harmony with the natural world and care for the plants and creatures of the woodland. He becomes, for a time, the archetypal Green Man of ancient myth and legend. The longer he embodies the Green Man, the more he takes on those sensibilities. When he returns to his former life he is a changed person, one who respects rather than exploits the resources of the natural world.

There are times when we do not recognize that we are changing; it is an unconscious process. We act as if we hold an identity and over time we authentically come to hold that identity. Sometimes we do not realize how we have changed—and been called to that change—until we are in a new setting.

### Opening to New Revelation

Revelation can sneak up on us while we are busy doing something else. The young squire has no sense that there is anything amiss with his exploitation of the natural world. The Green Man experience that opens up for him a new way of being is not one he seeks. However, when he finds himself confronted with a new reality, he allows himself to be taught. He embraces wholly the revelation that is thrust upon him, and lets it change his core being. Sometimes we, too, are caught unaware by events or circumstances that lead to new revelations. In embracing those unexpected, often difficult, experiences and allowing them to teach us, we grow our souls.

### Finding Wisdom Through the Principles and Sources

The Green Man's conversion comes about as a result of time spent alone in the woods, where he discovers the responsibility and the joy of cooperating with the natural world. This story reminds us of the writings of Henry David Thoreau, who spent two years living simply in a cabin in the woods at Walden Pond. Our Unitarian Universalist theology and tradition are deeply influenced by Thoreau's ideal of connection to the rhythm of the natural world. Unitarian Universalists who find experiences of wonder, awe, and the divine in nature, are echoing the ideas of earth-centered traditions and the writings of Thoreau.

## Connecting with Our Lives

### In Our Faith Communities

Engage children in a "Green Man" experience. It can be as simple as a walk in the woods to observe, smell, touch, and listen to what is there. Invite children and adults to share stories of their own adventures in the woods. How does it feel to be in the woods or sit in a nearby tree when we are upset or need to be alone? Invite sharing about these mini-retreats into nature. How are we changed by our connections with the natural world?

This story lends itself well to an intergenerational play. The Green Man is best played by an adult or teen, but there are many roles that children can play—woodland creatures, hunting companions, villagers, trees, and so on. Because the costuming can be fun and creative, the faith community can work on a Green Man play as a multiweek project.

## At Home

Camping in the woods can serve as a "Green Man" experience for children and families. It offers a different rhythm of life without the complexities of modern living. While camping, families can often experience more deeply and readily their connections with the interdependent web of life.

Children and families may enjoy viewing photos of Green Man carvings and statues found on a variety of Internet sites. If your family has a Green Man depiction in the garden, children will enjoy connecting it with the story. The Green Man is an ideal theme for creating visual art using clay or paper maché, or even materials as simple as paper, green paint, and torn green tissue for foliage.

# Conclusion

One autumn not long ago, as All Souls' Day grew near, I found myself torn about what story to tell as part of the worship service. For many years, I had told "The Mustard Seed Medicine" as part of the All Souls' worship for children, but that year I wondered about the wisdom of such a choice. The congregation I serve was grieving the death of a child, and I was not at all sure that I wanted to tell a story about a mother's grief following a child's death. I shared my concerns with a member of the congregation who is a good sounding board. Her response was to remind me that the recent loss in the congregation was exactly why I had developed an All Souls' liturgy for children that included the same story each year. The story was familiar enough to provide a container for the grief and for the questions that the children had about death. It reminds us that grief is a universal human experience; sometimes it is our turn to comfort, sometimes to be comforted.

When I told the story that year, the children listened as they always do, relaxing into a comfortable, familiar story, anticipating what would come next, shaking their heads with the neighbors who could not give the grieving mother what she requested. What followed surprised me. I expected conversation and many candles honoring the recent death that weighed so heavily on my spirit. Instead, there were candles and remembrances for grandparents, pets, beloved uncles, and a sister who had died several years earlier. Children brought to the story their own lived experiences and the things that weighed on their minds and spirits. The story touched each person differently and held wisdom that enabled each to be comforted and to grow in spirit.

As human beings, we seek meaning. In awe before the mysteries of life and love and the wonders of universe, we are not content until we make meaning of it all. Stories help us learn to respond to the challenges, joys, and wonders of being alive, and repeated stories touch us most deeply. They offer a container that can hold our hopes, dreams, fears, and sorrows at each age and stage of our lives. Whether a beloved story is from scripture, oral tradition, family lore, or from "for real" sources like biography or science, it is a wisdom story when it points us from the world of the story back to our own lived experience, growing our spirits in the process.

When we open our hearts and spirits to it, a wisdom story reveals its truth in layers, a bit at a time. It is in the dialogue between our experience and the world of the story that wisdom is found. Each time we remember or retell a particular story, we recall not only the story itself, but also the other times and circumstances when we heard, read, or told the story. More wisdom and more meaning are attached with each telling. The universal truth of the story and our own particular experiences with it reveal the story's meaning in our lives. The story becomes part of our spiritual toolkit, offering new revelation and new meaning as our lives unfold.

Unitarian Universalist faith calls us to carry our faith into the world, living in a way that brings more love and justice into our lives and the world. Finding our sense of calling is part of the spiritual journey. How can we offer our skills, talents, and love in the service of love and justice? Wisdom stories can help us discover, at each age and stage and in each moment of our lives, what it is that we are called to do. The journeys of folklore or scriptural heroes, the magnificence of the natural world, and the inspiration provided by the lives of prophets, teachers, explorers, and dreamers offer us ways to examine our own circumstances. Stories can help us discern and answer our particular calling in the service of something greater than ourselves.

Faith development for Unitarian Universalists lies in the interplay between lived experience and the sources of our tradition. We reflect on our experience in the light of wisdom from our Principles and Sources, carry our newfound wisdom into our lives, and grow in faith. Wisdom stories may open doors to new truths, but we must allow time and space for reflection and activities that connect each story with our own lives.

Not long ago, preteens in my congregation retold the story of David and Goliath. It is a story they have heard and worked with many times before. This time, however, the familiar story held something different for the group. As the story begins, David brings provisions to his brothers, who are soldiers in Saul's army. It is in the course of bringing these provisions that he hears Goliath's challenge. Instead of focusing on Goliath the giant and David the shepherd boy, this group focused on the experience of being at war. They talked about a cousin in Iraq and others they know who have family members fighting in a war. They used the wisdom story as a vehicle for examining their experience and for approaching a troubling topic. The following week, they made cards for a young adult parishioner away in the military, having a much stronger understanding of why sending the cards was a way to bring more love into the world. The interplay between a familiar wisdom story and their own lives led them to grow in understanding and spirit. When they reached out to offer love and compassion through their cards and notes, they were carrying their faith into the world in the very best tradition of Unitarian Universalism.

May we all find stories that sustain us, challenge us, and call us, each in our own way, to the work of bringing love and justice into the world.

# Bibliography

The stories in this collection are based on material from a variety of sources. Two stories ("We are All One" and "The Green Man") are adaptations of another's work. In all other cases, the tellings in this book are original, with themes, plots, characters, and motifs based on or inspired by ancient tales, biographical accounts, scientific writings, or historical material. Specific information follows about source material for each story and, in some cases, for the background information that helped in the framing of the tale.

*The Brementown Musicians*
Based on "The Travelling Musicians" in *The Brothers' Grimm Fairy Tales*, an English translation by Edgar Taylor and Marian Edwardes of *Kinder- und Hausmärchen* (*Nursery and Household Tales*) by Jacob and Wilhelm Grimm, published in two volumes in 1812 and 1814. The complete translated text is available online from Project Gutenberg.

*The Creation Story*
Based on Genesis Chapter 1, verses 1- 31 and Chapter 2, verses 1-3, in *The HarperCollins Study Bible: New Revised Standard Version*, edited by Wayne A. Meeks (HarperCollins, 1989).

*Jack and the Northwest Wind*
Based on "Jack and the Northwest Wind" in *The Jack Tales*, edited by Richard Chase (Houghton Mifflin, 1971), and "Jack and the Northwest Wind," in *The Jack Tales* by Ray Hicks (Callaway, 2000).

### The Lion's Whisker
Based on "Abegaz and the Lion" by Shannon Valencia, found on the Peace Corps World Wise Schools website, and "The Lion's Whisker," in *The Lion's Whisker and Other Ethiopian Tales*, edited by Brent Ashabranner and Russell Davis (Linnet, 1997).

### King of the Birds
Based on "King of the Birds," translated from an oral telling by Loreen McDonald. Background material from "Notes and Queries: 'Little King,' 'Sow,' 'Lady-Cow'" by Emily Hope Allen, in *Journal of American Folklore*, vol. 48, no. 188 (April-June 1935).

### Orfeo and Heurodis
Based on "The Imp Tree," in *Fairy Gold: A Book of Classic English Fairy Tales*, edited by Ernest Rhys (Hippocrene, 1999).

### We Are All One
Adapted from "We Are All One," in *The Rainbow People* by Lawrence Yep (HarperCollins, 1989) and "The Miracle Bead," in *The Golden Mountain: Chinese Tales Told in California*, collected by Jon Lee, edited by Paul Radin (California State Library, 1940). Background material from "Toward a Poetics of Asian American Fantasy: Lawrence Yep's Construction of a Bicultural Mythology" by Celestine Woo, in *The Lion and the Unicorn*, vol. 30 (2006).

### The Christmas Truce
Based on "Christmas in the Trenches, 1914" by Frank Richards, found on the EyeWitness to History website.

### For the Love of Stars
Based on *Cecilia Payne-Gaposchkin: An Autobiography and Other Recollections* by Katherine Haramundanis (Cambridge University Press, 1996).

*Rosa Parks*
Based on *Soul of a Citizen* by Paul Rogat Loeb (St. Martin's Griffin, 1999); "Mighty Times: The Legacy of Rosa Parks," found on the Teaching Tolerance website; and "Rosa Louise Parks Biography," found on the Rosa and Raymond Parks Institute for Self-Development website.

*Arius the Heretic*
Based on *When Jesus Became God* by Richard E. Rubenstein (Harcourt, Brace, 1999) and the Frontline television program *From Jesus to Christ: The First Christians* (WGBH Educational Foundation, 1998).

*The Mustard Seed Medicine*
Based on "The Mustard-Seed Medicine," in *From Long Ago and Many Lands: Stories for Children Told Anew* by Sophia Lyon Fahs (Skinner House, 1995).

*Abu Kassim's Shoes*
Based on "Abu Kassim's Boots," in *The Islamic Year: Surahs, Stories, and Celebration* by Noorah Al-Gailani and Chris Smith (Hawthorn, 2002) and "The Everlasting Slippers," in *The Book of the Thousand Nights and One Night*, vol. 3, translated by Dr. J.C. Mardrus and Powys Mathers (Routledge, 1964).

*The Call of Samuel*
Based on I Samuel 1:9-24, 3:1-21, 7:3-12, 8:4-22, and 10:1 in *The HarperCollins Study Bible, New Revised Standard Version*, edited by Wayne A. Meeks (HarperCollins, 1989), and *Introduction to the Old Testament: A Liberation Perspective* by Anthony R. Ceresko (Orbis, 1997).

*The Easter Story*
Based on Mark 1:21-45, 10:13-31, 12:28-34, 14:1-25, 14:32-42, 15:1-20, 15:42-46, 16:1-8, and 16:9-14 in *The HarperCollins Study*

*Bible: New Revised Standard Version*, edited by Wayne A. Meeks (HarperCollins, 1989).

*Charles Darwin*
Based on the "Darwin" exhibit, curated by Dr. Niles Eldridge, found on the American Museum of Natural History website; *Darwin: Discovering the Tree of Life* by Niles Eldridge (W.W. Norton, 2005); and *The Tree of Life* by Peter Sis (Farrar, Straus, Giroux, 2003).

*The Story of Sand*
Based on "Sands of the World" by Walter N. Mack and Elizabeth A. Leistikow, in *Scientific American,* vol. 275, no. 2 (August 1996); "How Many Grains of Sand Are in the World?" by Kristen Read, found on the Miami Museum of Science website; and "Team Traces Utah Desert Sand to Appalachian Mountains" by Jacqueline Weaver, in *Yale Bulletin and Calendar,* vol. 32, no. 4 (September 26, 2003).

*Nanabush and the Bulrushes*
Based on two different versions of "Nänabushu and the Dancing Bullrushes" as told by Wâsagunackank and Midasugnj in *Ojibwa Texts Collected by William Jones,* edited by Truman Michelson (1917), found in the Digital General Collection of the University of Michigan. Background information from *The Mishomis Book: The Voice of the Ojibway* by Edward Benton-Benai (Red School House, 1988); "Nanabush Stories from the Ojibway" by Ridi Wilson Ghezzi, in *Coming to Light: Contemporary Translations of the Native Literatures of North America,* edited by Brian Swann (Random House, 1994); "Is That All There Is? Tribal Literature" by Johnston Basil, in *An Anthology of Canadian Native Literature in English,* edited by Daniel David Moses and Terry Goldie (Oxford University Press, 1992); and *The Manitous: The Supernatural World of the Ojibway* by Basil Johnston (HarperCollins, 1995).

*The Green Man*
Adapted from *The Green Man* by Gail E. Haley (Charles Scribner's Sons, 1979). Background material from *Green Man: The Archetype of Our Oneness with the Earth* by William Anderson (Harper-Collins Publishers, 1990).

# Acknowledgments

I am grateful to those who helped this book move from idea to published work. I owe a special debt of gratitude to Dr. Tracey Hurd, who perceived the need for such a collection and asked me to write it. She served throughout the process as developmental editor, guiding and supporting the project as it moved along. Barbara Gifford helped with copyright research. Marie Houck provided a critical sounding board and accountability relationship as I worked to better understand Anishinabe culture.

My deep thanks are owed also to those who, over the years, have challenged me and helped me develop an understanding of how to approach wisdom stories in a way that respects the cultures from which they come, including the members of the Liberal Religious Educators Association Integrity Team. I was cheered on throughout the writing process by the members, staff, children, and youth of the North Parish of North Andover, Massachusetts, and by my own beloved family, husband Stephen, and young adult children Stephanie, Heather, and Owen. I am grateful for their constant and unending support!